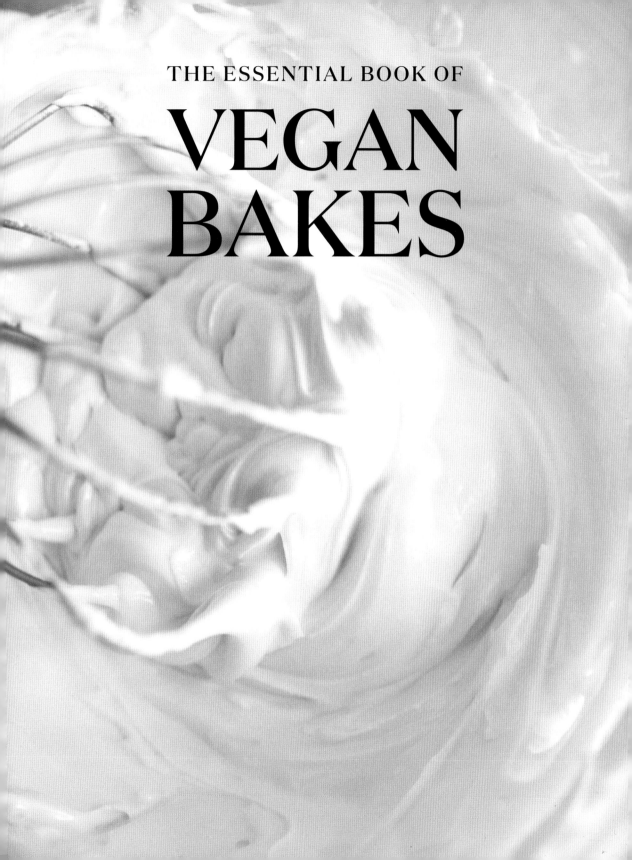

THE ESSENTIAL BOOK OF
VEGAN
BAKES

THE ESSENTIAL BOOK OF

VEGAN BAKES

Irresistible Plant-Based Cakes and Treats

HOLLY JADE

CREATOR OF *THE LITTLE BLOG OF VEGAN*

Countryman Press

An Imprint of W. W. Norton & Company
Independent Publishers Since 1923

Chocolate Caramel Brownie Cups, page 167

CONTENTS

Introduction

I am so excited to bring you my very first vegan baking book. I made a book! I still can't believe it. It's been an absolute pleasure to work on this, and I want to thank every single person who has helped me bring it to life and all of you for buying it.

I have many happy childhood memories centered around baking and creating a mess in my family kitchen, and I wanted to produce a book filled with delicious classic and unique baked goods and desserts that everyone can enjoy—vegan and non-vegan alike.

I am incredibly proud of every single recipe in this book and have worked especially hard to create recipes that suit all abilities, using ingredients that most people will recognize. If you love desserts and sweet treats, then you've come to the right place. *The Essential Book of Vegan Bakes* welcomes you to the world of vegan baking!

The Story So Far

My name is Holly Jade, and I'm the founder, owner, and creator of *The Little Blog of Vegan*, a multi-award-winning vegan food blog, where I share all of my tasty recipe creations and drool-worthy food photography (if I do say so myself!).

To understand how I got to where I am now, I have to reflect back on my school days. I had a very low school attendance record due to school phobia and health problems. I left school with very few job prospects, no plans for the future, and no desire to return to an educational setting because of the difficult time I'd had. I had hoped that leaving school would be a relief, but instead I suffered from depression. It was an extremely upsetting time for me, and it was also around this time that I started to develop intolerances to certain foods. As a result, I had to go on a strict exclusion diet.

During this time, my wonderful cat and best friend, Tiggs, was a great comfort to me. Honestly, he became a treasured part of my life, and that is why I dedicated this book to him. He recently passed away after spending 18 cherished years by my side. It was thanks to his companionship that I decided I couldn't continue to support the meat and dairy industries, knowing how much harm they cause to innocent, beautiful animals just like my Tiggs. So I began to eat a plant-based diet, and I stopped wearing or using any products that came from an animal or that had been tested on animals.

I spent many hours researching foods that were vegan and cruelty-free, and I wanted to share my findings with others. That's when my sister, Naomi, suggested I start a vegan food blog, and so *The Little Blog of Vegan* was born. Not only did creating my blog help me through a very difficult period in my life but I was also able to develop it into a full-time business that went on to win prestigious awards. Most importantly, it has enabled me to do what I love for a living. I still find it hard to believe that my blog has led me to work alongside high-profile international companies. I'm especially proud of my Instagram account, @thelittleblogofvegan, which has helped me to evolve my style and grow an organic audience of followers from all over the world.

Not bad for a girl who left school without a clue!

The Story Continues

Though my blog started as a general vegan food blog, over time I became more passionate about baking, which is something I loved to do as a child with my mom. I love the freedom it gives me to express my imagination through my creations. Some of my favorite recipes include my cute hedgehog doughnuts, polar bear cupcakes, reindeer tartlets, themed celebration cakes, and bakery-style desserts (see pages 214–215 for photos of some of these creations).

I am happiest when I'm in the kitchen, baking and experimenting with new recipes, but my other passions are food styling, photography, videography, and editing. Everything I do, I have taught myself—from building a popular website to recipe creating, running a business, managing social media channels, and liaising with influential companies. It goes to show that you don't have to invest in further education if you have dreams, passion, and faith in yourself. My business isn't just a job to me, it's a massive part of my life and something I love and feel passionate about. My followers are exceptional and have always been so supportive throughout my journey—I have even met other awesome creators I now regard as friends. Whenever a follower makes one of my recipes and shares it on Instagram, it makes my day. I just want to encourage and inspire other people to bake—after all, a cake will brighten up anyone's day.

There is no end to my blogging journey. Something fresh is always around the corner, and not a day goes by that there isn't something new to do or to plan for. I have to pinch myself sometimes when I remember that my work is not only being recognized around the world but is valued as well! I've had my recipes featured on the front cover of magazines, and over the last few years I have won awards, including Blogosphere's "Food Blogger of the Year," been named a "Top Ten Baking Blog" by Vuelio, been a finalist in PETA's Great Vegan Bake-Off, and been shortlisted for Pinterest's Food and Drink Awards. How amazing is that?!

Creating this book is yet another incredible opportunity. Who'd have thought that I would be writing my very own baking book? I am so thankful to Countryman Press for sharing my vision and having faith in me and my work.

I wanted to share my story with you, as well as my bakes and creations, as it's extremely important to me to convey that even when things seem hopeless, achieving your goals— and your dream job—is possible if you just believe in yourself.

Holly Jade x

Equipment

When it comes to creating the most delicious baked goods and desserts, you don't need expensive, top-of-the-line utensils. Sometimes simple, basic tools work just as well. Here's a list of what's in my kitchen and the utensils I use regularly.

KITCHEN SCALE One of my most-used and crucial kitchen tools is my trusty digital scale. I prefer digital scales because they're more precise and easy to use, and they're great for making sure the bake comes out perfect each time.

CAKE PANS There are so many kinds out there. I prefer to use removable-bottom or springform cake pans, as they make it easier to turn the cakes out once baked. Make sure you're using the correct cake pan for the cake you're making. If your pan is too shallow, the cake batter could overflow, causing a mess in your oven and a very flat cake. My most-used cake pan sizes are 6-inch (15 cm), 8-inch (20 cm), and 10-inch (25 cm) pans with removable bottoms. If you want to create layered cakes, it's worth investing in a few pans of the same size to save on baking time. I also find it helpful to have a variety of differently sized loaf pans, pie pans, tartlet pans, and muffin or cupcake pans. It is vital to have a muffin or cupcake pan when making cupcakes to hold the liners in place.

BAKING SHEETS Large, flat, metal baking sheets are essential if you plan on making a lot of cookies. It's best to have at least two.

MEASURING SPOONS You can buy these as a set—they are a kitchen must-have.

MEASURING CUPS I find weighing food in metric or imperial much more accurate than measuring the volume of an ingredient in cups or spoons, but for the benefit of my lovely followers in the US and Canada, I have included cup measurements alongside the metric weights. Unless otherwise stated, cup measurements are for level cups.

A SELECTION OF PIPING BAGS AND PIPING TIPS These are used for decorating cakes, cookies, and desserts with buttercream, frosting, whipped cream, or royal icing. You can buy a whole range of piping tips, from pastry nozzles to large round nozzles, but my most-used piping tip has to be the 2D closed star nozzle, which I use to create different effects. You can buy reusable piping bags to reduce waste, or biodegradable bags that can be composted.

SPATULAS I have a variety of spatulas for different jobs. For example, I use small and large spatulas for spreading buttercream, an offset spatula (or angled palette knife) for frosting cakes, a large slotted spatula for flipping doughnuts in oil, and a rubber spatula for mixing, spreading, and scraping.

CAKE SCRAPER This is a metal instrument used to scrape the buttercream on the side of your cake to give it a smooth, professional look. You can get decorative cake scrapers for adding texture to your buttercream.

SMALL AND LARGE SIEVES These are required to sift dry ingredients to break up any lumps, and to combine and aerate ingredients. Sifting confectioners' sugar helps to create a smoother buttercream or frosting. I use a small sieve to sift confectioners' sugar over desserts to decorate them.

STAND MIXER Stand mixers aren't always essential, but they're great time-savers, and many freestanding mixers come with a variety of attachments. If you are serious about baking, it's worth investing in a good-quality stand mixer. I love the balloon-whisk attachment, which is perfect for creating buttercream, frosting, and meringue. The dough hook is excellent for creating doughnut and bread dough, and the flat paddle attachment is ideal for mixing ingredients that require less air to be incorporated—for example, when you are beating butter and sugar together.

BLENDER OR FOOD PROCESSOR I prefer to use my blender for whizzing up creamy cheesecake fillings, but a food processor can also be used for this and similar jobs.

ELECTRIC HAND MIXER You can use an electric hand mixer in place of a stand mixer or blender for most things. You can use a hand mixer as well, but you will have to work harder and it will take you longer.

SPOONS This may seem obvious, but they're vital and so need a mention. I have a variety of spoons in my kitchen, ranging from the classic wooden spoon to metal and silicone spoons. Wooden spoons are a great all-rounder for mixing, and they don't conduct heat like metal spoons. Silicone spoons are great, as they come in lots of different shapes and sizes—some of them have a rounded edge, which I prefer for folding different ingredients together while incorporating air.

CANDY THERMOMETER I use a candy thermometer to measure the correct temperature when I am frying doughnuts and tempering chocolate. You don't always need a thermometer, but it will help you reach the exact temperature you require.

ICE CREAM SCOOP This is great for measuring the exact amount of batter in cupcakes (as well as for scooping ice cream).

CAKE TURNTABLE If you're serious about cake decorating, this is a must-have piece of equipment. Place the undecorated cake on the turntable, load on the buttercream or frosting, and rotate the turntable while scraping to make the frosting even.

MICROPLANE/FINE GRATER This is ideal for finely grating lemon, lime, and orange zest, as well as for creating shavings of chocolate.

ROLLING PIN Not only can this be used to roll out and shape dough, but you can also use one to crush cookies if you don't have a food processor.

BOWLS Another obvious one, but it's really important to have a wide selection of bowls, ranging from small bowls for royal icing to large ones for mixing batter for cakes and other desserts. I also have a selection of heatproof bowls for using as a bain-marie to melt chocolate.

BLOWTORCH Although not essential, I use my blowtorch for toasting meringues, flame-roasting s'mores and marshmallows, softening chocolate, and caramelizing fruit.

COOKIE CUTTERS It's good to have a selection of cookie cutters. The classic round, square, and heart-shaped cutters are really useful to have, and festive cookie cutters are great to use during the holidays for things like gingerbread men.

COOLING RACK/WIRE RACK I use these to cool cakes and desserts when they come out of the oven. They help air flow around the cakes, enabling them to cool faster. They also help to protect your worktop from hot cake pans and baking sheets!

PUTTY KNIFE This is an industrial tool with a flat and flexible knife blade. I find this is an extremely useful tool in the process of tempering chocolate and creating chocolate curls, as in my recipe on page 36.

Key Ingredients

Here are the ingredients that I use most often for the recipes in this book. This should give you an idea of what ingredients are generally required in vegan baking and desserts.

FLOURS Self-rising flour is used for cakes, as it has an added rising agent. For bakes that don't require a rising agent, such as cookies and pastries, all-purpose flour is preferred.

RISING AGENTS These agents produce carbon dioxide when baking, which makes the cakes rise. The two that I use most regularly are baking powder and baking soda.

YEAST This is a rising agent used in making bread. I include it in my recipes for doughnuts (pages 90 and 94), cinnamon rolls (page 76), and hot cross buns (page 84). I prefer to use active dry yeast in my recipes.

SUGARS The main sugars I use in my baking are superfine sugar, light and dark brown sugars, and confectioners' sugar. Superfine sugar is ideal for cakes, meringues, and caramel sauce. Golden superfine sugar is an unrefined form of superfine sugar, which I sometimes prefer to use in cakes, but white superfine sugar works just as well. Light and dark brown sugars contain molasses and are ideal for adding a caramel flavor, for example in gingerbread cookies. Confectioners'

sugar (you can also use powdered sugar) is known as icing sugar in the UK.

SYRUPS Maple syrup is a natural sweetener derived from the maple tree and is ideal for my raspberry crumble bars (page 141) and drizzling over pancakes (page 169). Golden syrup is made by refining sugarcane, and is slightly thicker than maple syrup, with a caramel flavor; I use it in flapjacks (pages 112 and 114). Black treacle is made from molasses and has a stronger, slightly bitter flavor, so it is ideal in gingerbread recipes (page 147). If you can't get hold of golden syrup or black treacle, you can try light or dark corn syrup as alternatives.

COCOA AND CACAO POWDER Cocoa powder is created by fermenting, drying, and roasting cacao beans and then grinding them. Cacao powder is purer and made without roasting but is not as sweet as cocoa powder. Both are ideal for adding a chocolate flavor to buttercream and many of my desserts and cakes.

DAIRY-FREE CHOCOLATE There are a range of dairy-free chocolates on the market with varying degrees of cocoa content. The higher the cocoa content, the more bitter the chocolate taste. The more cocoa butter in the chocolate, the creamier the chocolate will taste. I have suggested using chocolate with a higher cocoa content in some recipes. For example, in the chocolate mousse pots (page 170), I suggest using chocolate with at least 70% cocoa content, as it just works better. Chocolate measurements given in cups are for chocolate chips, unless specified otherwise in the recipe.

CREAM OF TARTAR This is a powdery, acidic by-product of fermenting grapes and is used as a stabilizer in recipes. It helps to create those famous peaks in meringues.

DAIRY-FREE MILK There are many plant-based milks on the market—for example, rice, oat, soy, almond, and cashew milk. My preferred milks to use in cake and dough-based recipes are soy and almond milk, but other milks will still work well. Dairy-free condensed milk comes in a can and is thicker and sweeter than ordinary milk. It works well in my lemon curd (page 197). Most supermarkets sell at least one dairy-free brand.

DAIRY-FREE BUTTER/MARGARINE There is now a decent selection of dairy-free butters on the market. Sticks or blocks of butter, like those from Miyoko's and Earth Balance brands, are ideal for my swiss meringue buttercream recipe on page 198.

DAIRY-FREE CREAM CHEESE I use cream cheese in frosting and cheesecakes. Most supermarkets will stock a brand of vegan cream cheese that uses coconut oil and soy in the ingredients. Violife offers a soy-free alternative.

DAIRY-FREE CREAM There are several dairy-free cream alternatives available, made with oats, soy, or coconut. Any of these are good to use in my caramel sauce on page 204 and chocolate ganache on page 48, for example.

DAIRY-FREE WHIPPING CREAM You can get hold of coconut-based whipping cream in most supermarkets, and it's ideal for adding decoration, as well as providing extra taste and creaminess, to desserts. The brand Silk makes a soy-based whipping cream.

COCONUT CREAM This is much thicker and richer than coconut milk, as it has a higher fat content. Many of my recipes use coconut cream to, for example, provide a nice creaminess to cheesecakes—see my no-bake strawberry cheesecake (page 183)—and coconut macaroons (page 124). Most supermarkets sell a brand of coconut cream or milk. For the recipes in this book, cans of coconut milk should be premium and full fat. You can separate out the cream from a can of premium-quality, full-fat coconut milk. To do this, tip the can upside down before fully opening it and pour out the watery fluid, leaving you with the cream. This tends to work better if you chill the can in the fridge beforehand.

TOFU This is a vegan protein source made of condensed soy milk. For this book, I use silken tofu, as it has a smooth consistency that is ideal for use in cheesecakes (and it can be eaten raw, which makes it perfect for no-bake cheesecakes). Just make sure you drain it well.

EGG REPLACEMENTS There are many different vegan options for replacing eggs in baking, but here are a few that I use in this book:

- **Apple cider vinegar:** My preferred egg replacement in cakes. Apple cider vinegar helps to activate baking powder and baking soda.

- **Banana:** You can sub one ripe mashed banana for every egg needed in a recipe. Bananas are great for my lava cakes (page 51).

- **Aquafaba:** The starchy liquid found in a can of chickpeas, although some companies now sell aquafaba as a product on its own. Generally, 3 tablespoons of aquafaba will bind ingredients as a whole egg would. I use it in meringues and mousses, as it magically whips up to create a creamy, fluffy foam.

- **Applesauce:** Apples contain pectin, which has great binding properties, and that is why applesauce makes a good egg replacement. I use it in my hot cross buns (page 84).

- **Flax "eggs":** There is gum in flaxseed/linseed that becomes jelly-like when mixed with water and helps strengthen the structure of baked goods, acting in a similar way to eggs. To make one flax egg, add 1 tablespoon of milled flaxseed/linseed to 3 tablespoons of water, let it sit for 10 minutes, and you've got a great egg substitute to use in baked goods like doughnuts (pages 90 and 94).

FOOD FLAVORINGS These are great when you want to enhance a flavor without affecting the texture of your dessert. Vanilla enhances all the other flavors in baking. I prefer to use vanilla extract, as it is less processed than vanilla essence. You can go all out and use pure vanilla from vanilla bean pods, but they are quite expensive. I also use orange, peppermint, and almond extracts in my recipes.

FOOD COLORING Make sure you are using vegan-friendly food coloring, as some aren't. I prefer to use gel food coloring rather than liquid, as it has more pigment and doesn't affect the texture of the dessert when added. You also don't need to add as much, which makes it more cost-effective.

Other Baking Tips

- Always read the recipe to the end before you start. Get out all the ingredients and check that you have the time and equipment you need.

- Always follow the method carefully and make sure you measure and weigh your ingredients accurately. Double-check that you have included all your ingredients as you go along.

- Use an oven thermometer to make sure your oven functions at the correct temperature.

- When baking cakes, don't open the oven door too early or the cake may sink in the middle.

- Don't put too many baking sheets or cakes into the oven at any one time, as they may cook unevenly. If the recipe says to use the middle of the oven, then do just that and bake the different cakes or sheets one at a time.

- Don't store cakes and cookies in the same container, as the moisture from the cake will soften the cookies.

- Undecorated cakes and cookies can be frozen, then defrosted at a later date and decorated.

- To ensure you have evenly sized layers in a layered cake, weigh the full amount of cake mixture and divide it by however many cake layers you require.

- To make sure you have a flat surface on a cake before decorating, turn over the top cake so the flat base is on the top. Another option is to use a sharp serrated knife and carefully cut off the dome of the cake, making sure that the knife is completely parallel to the kitchen worktop, leaving you with an even surface.

- When making bread, doughnuts, or any other dough-based bake, it's important to knead the dough to the right consistency. This can be done with a stand mixer fitted with a dough-hook attachment, but I prefer to do it by hand on a lightly floured surface, as it's easier to feel when the dough is ready. Under-kneaded dough is loose and won't rise properly when baked; over-kneaded dough can become dense and tough and results in a hard loaf/bake. You want the dough to be smooth, elastic, and to hold its shape.

- When a recipe asks you to "fold in" ingredients, use a spatula or sharp-edged spoon to carefully fold the mixture around the edges of the bowl and into the middle, then repeat. Do this gently, without stirring or whisking. You want to combine the mixture and trap the air in it, which makes for a lighter consistency.

- I'd recommend having more than one baking sheet, especially when it comes to baking cookies, so you can make multiple batches without having to disturb any cookies while they cool on the sheet. Also, using a hot baking sheet just out of the oven may affect the baking time and the end result of the next batch.

- A bain-marie is used to melt ingredients gently, without burning. To melt chocolate in a bain-marie, add a small amount of water to a pan and place a heatproof bowl on top with the chocolate inside. Turn the heat to medium, and the steam will melt the chocolate.

- Before baking your cake, I advise using parchment paper to line the pan. This helps to stop the cake from sticking to the pan, and it also helps to prevent the sides and bottom of the cake from becoming overbaked. To line a round cake pan, you will need to cut out a circle of parchment paper to fit the base. You can do this by drawing around the base of the pan and then cutting the circle out slightly inside the line. Then cut strips of parchment to go around the inside of the pan. The strips should be the same depth as the pan, making sure there are no gaps. Grease the pan with dairy-free butter or margarine before lining to help the paper stay in place.

To line a loaf pan or square cake pan that doesn't have a loose base, grease the base and sides of the pan with dairy-free butter or margarine to keep the parchment paper in place. Lay some parchment paper on a kitchen worktop and place the pan on top. Measure a strip that's the same length as the base but wide enough to cover the base and the long sides of the pan, with an extra ¾ inch (2 cm) on each side. Cut out the strip of paper and lay it inside the pan, covering the base and long sides with an overhang on each side. Rub some dairy-free butter or margarine on top of the parchment paper, then cut another strip of parchment paper big enough to cover the base and shorter sides of the pan, with the same ¾-inch (2 cm) overhang on each side. This makes it easier to pull the bake out when it is ready to remove from the pan.

To line a baking sheet, cut the parchment paper to the size needed and secure with some dairy-free butter or margarine.

- After baking, leave the cake to cool slightly before attempting to remove it from the pan. After about 10 minutes, carefully run a knife around the edge of the cake on the outside of the parchment paper to make sure it hasn't stuck, then place the cooling rack over the cake and flip the cake upside down. Gently tap the base of the pan to loosen the cake, then carefully take off the parchment paper and allow the cake to cool fully. For baking pans without a loose base and loaf pans, wait for the bake to cool slightly, then lift it out using the parchment paper and place on a cooling rack. Allow to cool fully before removing the parchment paper.

CAKES AND CUPCAKES

Victoria Sponge Cake

I've taken the classic English Victoria sponge cake and given it a zesty twist: layers of lemon-flavored sponge filled with strawberry jam and vanilla cream frosting, and topped with fresh strawberries and a dusting of confectioners' sugar. If you needed an excuse to throw a tea party, this is it.

Serves 14–16

Cakes
- 2 cups (480 ml) dairy-free milk
- 2 teaspoons apple cider vinegar
- 3¾ cups (470 g) self-rising flour
- 1¾ cups (350 g) superfine sugar
- 1 teaspoon baking powder
- 1 teaspoon baking soda
- ½ cup (120 ml) sunflower oil
- 1 teaspoon vanilla extract
- Zest of 1 medium lemon

Frosting
- 4 tablespoons (¼ cup; 60 g) butter/margarine
- 2 tablespoons cream cheese
- 3⅓ cups (400 g) confectioners' sugar, sifted
- ½ teaspoon vanilla extract
- Dash of dairy-free milk, if needed

- 4 tablespoons strawberry jam (see my berry jam recipe on page 203)
- Handful of strawberries
- Dusting of confectioners' sugar (optional)

CAKES

1. Preheat the oven to 400°F (200°C) and line two 8-inch (20 cm) round removable-bottom cake pans with parchment paper (see page 17 for how to line a cake pan). If you only have one, you will have to bake the cakes separately. Just remember to cover the batter with a tea towel and give it a quick stir before baking the second cake.

2. In a bowl, whisk the milk with the apple cider vinegar until fully combined. Set aside for 10 minutes to curdle—this creates a vegan buttermilk.

3. In a large mixing bowl, sift the flour, superfine sugar, baking powder, and baking soda. Mix well to combine. Add the oil to the buttermilk and whisk to combine.

4. Add the buttermilk mixture, vanilla extract, and lemon zest to the dry ingredients and mix with a wooden spoon.

5. Divide the cake batter equally between the lined cake pans. Tap the pans on the worktop a few times to remove any air bubbles. Pop the cakes into the center of the oven and bake for around 35–40 minutes (checking at 35 minutes). You will know they are done when they are springy to the touch and a knife or skewer inserted into the center comes out clean.

6. Remove the cakes from the oven, place on a cooling rack, and allow to cool slightly before removing them from the pans (see page 17 for a tip on how to remove cakes from their pans). Put the cakes on the rack to cool fully. Once cool, pop them into a sealed container to keep them fresh before frosting.

Recipe continued on page 22

HOLLY'S TIP

The cakes can
be stored in a sealed
container and frosted
the following day.

HOLLY'S TIP

Add the
fresh strawberries
just before serving
to prevent the cake
from becoming
too moist.

FROSTING

1. In a bowl or stand mixer, cream the butter or margarine and cream cheese together on high, then add the confectioners' sugar and vanilla extract. Whip until smooth and well combined, adding a dash of milk if needed. As this is a naked cake, the frosting needs to be quite thick to keep it stable.

2. Transfer the frosting to a piping bag fitted with a large round-tip nozzle.

3. Pipe a thin layer of frosting over one of the cakes, leaving a 1-inch (2.5 cm) border. Spread the strawberry jam over the top of the frosting and cover with some of the chopped fresh strawberries.

4. Pipe a decorative border around the edge of the jam and strawberry layer, then place the other cake on top. To make the filling more decorative, add some jam to a piping bag and pipe in between the frosting (see photo on page 20).

5. Pipe decorative frosting on top of the cake and decorate with fresh strawberries (see Tip). Finish with a dusting of confectioners' sugar, if using.

Store in the fridge in a sealed container. Best eaten within a few days. Leave at room temperature for 15 minutes before serving.

Carrot Cake

I'm not sure if this counts as one of your five a day, but I love a slice of classic carrot cake. My vegan carrot cake recipe features a moist and mildly spiced carrot sponge with a smooth, sweet cream topping—extremely delicious and makes the perfect pairing with a hot cup of coffee or an afternoon tea. *See photo on page 25.*

Serves 18–20

Cakes
- 2 cups (480 ml) dairy-free milk
- 2 teaspoons apple cider vinegar
- ½ cup (50 g) walnuts
- 3⅓ cups plus 1 tablespoon (425 g) self-rising flour
- 2¼ cups (450 g) superfine sugar
- 1 teaspoon baking powder
- 1 teaspoon baking soda
- 1 tablespoon ground cinnamon
- 1 teaspoon ground nutmeg
- 1⅓ cups (150 g) carrots, peeled and grated
- ½ cup (120 g) sunflower oil

Frosting
- ⅔ cup (150 g) dairy-free butter/margarine
- 2 tablespoons dairy-free cream cheese
- ½ teaspoon vanilla extract
- 5 cups (600 g) confectioners' sugar, sifted
- Dash of dairy-free milk, if needed

- ½ cup plus 2 tablespoons (80 g) walnuts, roughly chopped, to decorate
- 1 carrot, peeled, to decorate
- Mint sprig, to decorate

CAKES

1. Preheat the oven to 400°F (200°C) and line three 8-inch (20 cm) round cake pans with parchment paper (see my tips on page 17 for lining cake pans). If you don't have three pans you will have to bake the cakes separately—keep the mixing bowl covered with a tea towel between bakes and stir the batter before use.

2. In a bowl, whisk the milk with the apple cider vinegar until fully combined. Set aside for 10 minutes to curdle—this creates vegan buttermilk.

3. Place the walnuts in a blender and blend them until finely ground.

4. In a large mixing bowl, sift the flour, superfine sugar, baking powder, baking soda, ground cinnamon, and ground nutmeg. Add the grated carrot and ground walnuts. Mix well to combine.

5. Add the oil to the buttermilk and whisk to combine. Pour this mixture into the other cake ingredients and mix.

6. Divide the cake batter equally among the lined cake pans. Tap the pans on the worktop a few times to remove any air bubbles.

7. Pop the cakes into the center of the oven and bake for around 28–30 minutes. You will know they are done when they are springy to the touch and a knife or skewer inserted into the center of the cakes comes out clean.

8. Remove the cakes from the oven, place on a cooling rack, and allow them to cool slightly before removing them from the pans (see page 17 for how to remove a cake from its pan). Once cool, pop them into a sealed container to keep them fresh before frosting.

Recipe continued on page 24

FROSTING

1. In a bowl or stand mixer, cream the butter or margarine, cream cheese, and vanilla extract together on high speed until smooth and creamy. Add the confectioners' sugar and whisk until the frosting is light and fluffy. You can do this by hand, but it will take you longer. If the frosting is too thick, add a dash of milk; if it's too wet, add more confectioners' sugar. You'll use the frosting for filling the cake, the crumb coat, and the final coat.

2. Place the first cake layer on a cake turntable, serving plate, or cake board. Frost the top and place the second cake layer on top, then repeat until all 3 layers of cake are sandwiched together with frosting. Using a palette knife, crumb-coat the whole cake (see page 212 for how to crumb-coat a cake). After applying the crumb coat, place the cake in the fridge for an hour to allow the crumb coat to set firm—this makes it easier to apply the final coat of frosting.

3. Once firm, add a thicker layer of frosting to the whole cake using a palette knife. Smooth out the frosting on the sides and top of the cake using a cake scraper or a palette knife (see page 212 for how to apply the final coat).

4. Using a spoon or spatula, create a swirl effect on the top of the cake. You may wish to add more frosting to the top of the cake to create more swirls (this is optional). Press the chopped walnuts to the sides of the cake in an ombre effect (i.e., with more at the bottom and fewer as you go up the cake).

5. Take the carrot and carve it into the shape of two mini carrots. Use a knife to make incisions in the side of the carrots to make them look more authentic. Make a hole in the top of the mini carrots and pop in a small sprig of mint or other similar herb. I used a toothpick to make one of the carrots stand upright.

This is best enjoyed within a few days of making. Store leftover cake in a sealed container in the fridge and leave at room temperature for 20 minutes before serving.

Lemon Loaf Cake

I've always loved lemon drizzle cakes: moist, zesty, and sweet, with a sticky topping that I can't get enough of. This is the perfect tea-time crowd-pleaser.

Serves 8–10

Loaf
- 2¼ cups (275 g) self-rising flour
- 1 teaspoon baking powder
- ¾ cup plus 2½ tablespoons (195 g) superfine sugar
- 1 medium lemon, zest and juice
- ⅓ cup plus 1½ tablespoons (100 ml) sunflower oil
- ¾ cup (170 ml) water

Icing
- 1 cup (120 g) confectioners' sugar, sifted
- 2 tablespoons lemon juice
- Lemon zest, to decorate (optional)

HOLLY'S TIP
Sometimes there may be a slight dip in the top of the cake. If that happens, tip the cake upside down while it's still warm so the top is facing down.

LOAF

1. Preheat the oven to 400°F (200°C) and line a 9-by-5-inch (23 by 13 cm) loaf pan with parchment paper (see page 17 for how to line a loaf pan). Allow the paper to hang on either side of the pan so it is easier to remove the loaf when baked. In a large mixing bowl, stir together the flour, baking powder, superfine sugar, and lemon zest. In a separate bowl, combine the oil, water, and lemon juice.

2. Pour the wet mixture into the dry and mix with a wooden spoon until combined. Pour the cake batter evenly into the lined pan. Tap the pan a few times to release any air bubbles.

3. Place the pan in the middle of the oven and bake for 30–35 minutes, or until golden brown. You will know it's done when it is springy to the touch and a knife or skewer inserted into the center comes out clean. Once baked, remove the loaf from the oven and allow to cool slightly before lifting out of the pan. Place on a cooling rack with the parchment paper and leave to cool fully before removing the paper. Place the cake on a serving dish/plate.

ICING

1. Place the confectioners' sugar in a bowl and add the lemon juice. Whisk together (a hand mixer is fine for this). Spread the icing over the cake using a spatula or spoon and let it drizzle down the sides. Sprinkle over lemon zest, if using.

Best served fresh and eaten within a few days of making. Store in a sealed container in the fridge and leave at room temperature for 20 minutes before serving.

Coffee and Walnut Loaf Cake

Coffee and walnuts go together like Buzz and Woody: vastly different yet the perfect match! This loaf is rich, with the sweet and nutty taste of the walnuts and a coffee kick that's further accentuated by the creamy coffee frosting.

Serves 8–10

Loaf
- 1¾ cups plus 2¾ tablespoons (240 g) all-purpose flour
- 1 tablespoon cocoa powder
- 2 teaspoons baking powder
- 2½ tablespoons dark brown sugar
- ⅓ cup plus 1 tablespoon (80 g) superfine sugar
- 3 tablespoons ground instant coffee
- 5 tablespoons (70 ml) sunflower oil
- ½ teaspoon apple cider vinegar
- ¾ cup plus 2½ tablespoons (220 ml) dairy-free milk
- ⅓ cup (40 g) walnuts, roughly chopped

Frosting
- ⅓ cup plus 1 tablespoon (90 g) dairy-free cream cheese
- 2 cups plus 1 tablespoon (250 g) confectioners' sugar, sifted
- 2 teaspoons ground instant coffee
- ¼ teaspoon boiling water

- Walnuts, roughly chopped, for decorating (optional)

LOAF

1. Preheat the oven to 375°F (195°C) and line a 9-by-5-inch (23 by 13 cm) deep loaf pan with parchment paper (see page 17 for how to line a loaf pan).

2. Sift the flour, cocoa powder, and baking powder into a large bowl. Add the sugars and the instant coffee, and stir to combine using a wooden spoon.

3. In a separate bowl, whisk together the oil, apple cider vinegar, and milk (a hand mixer will do the job!). Pour the wet ingredients over the dry and whisk until just combined (don't overwhisk, or the batter may become tough). Fold in the walnuts.

4. Pour the cake batter into the lined pan and use a spatula to spread it into the corners of the pan. Bake for around 40–45 minutes, or until a skewer inserted into the center comes out clean.

5. When the loaf is baked, carefully remove it from the oven and place it on a cooling rack in its pan for 5 minutes. Remove the cake from the pan and place on a cooling rack with the parchment paper. Leave to cool fully before removing the paper and then place the cake on a serving dish/plate.

FROSTING

1. Place the cream cheese in a medium mixing bowl and whip until creamy—you can use an electric hand mixer or a stand mixer with a balloon-whisk attachment.

Recipe continued on page 30

2. Sift in the confectioners' sugar and beat until thick and creamy. Put the coffee into a small bowl and pour over the boiling water. Stir to make a coffee concentrate. Pour this into the frosting and whisk together until incorporated. If the frosting is too runny, add more confectioners' sugar until it's thick and creamy.

3. Place the frosting in the fridge while the loaf cools. Give it an extra whip once it comes out of the fridge, as it can become firm. Spread the frosting over the top of the loaf, smoothing it out with the back of a spoon or a small spatula. Sprinkle over some walnuts, if using.

4. Place the loaf in the fridge for 30 minutes—doing this helps the cake and frosting set, making the loaf less crumbly when sliced. Use a serrated knife to slice it into servings.

This is best eaten within a few days of making. Store in a sealed container in the fridge and leave at room temperature for 20 minutes before serving.

Red Velvet Cake

Three tiers of sumptuous red velvet sponge with a mild chocolate flavor and buttery cream cheese frosting—this cake is true decadence. I highly recommend using a bright and vividly hued gel food coloring (rather than a liquid food coloring) when baking cakes to add that pop of color to the sponge without compromising the taste and texture of the bake. *See photo on page 33.*

Serves around 12

Cakes
- 2 cups (480 ml) dairy-free milk
- 2 teaspoons apple cider vinegar
- 3⅓ cups (420 g) self-rising flour
- 2 tablespoons cocoa powder
- 2 cups (400 g) superfine sugar
- 1 teaspoon baking powder
- 1 teaspoon baking soda
- ½ cup (120 ml) sunflower oil
- ½ teaspoon red gel food coloring

Frosting
- ⅔ cup (150 g) dairy-free butter/margarine
- ⅓ cup plus ½ tablespoon (80 g) dairy-free cream cheese
- 5 cups (600 g) confectioners' sugar, sifted
- 1 teaspoon vanilla extract

CAKES

1. Preheat the oven to 400°F (200°C) and line three 6-inch (15 cm) round removable-bottom cake pans with parchment paper (see page 17 for how to line a cake pan). If you don't have three pans, you will have to bake the cakes separately. Keep the mixing bowl covered with a tea towel between bakes and stir the cake batter before use.

2. In a bowl, whisk the milk with the apple cider vinegar until fully combined. Set aside for 10 minutes to curdle—this creates a vegan buttermilk.

3. In a large mixing bowl, sift the flour, cocoa powder, superfine sugar, baking powder, and baking soda. Mix well to combine.

4. Add the oil and gel food coloring to the buttermilk and whisk to combine. Add the wet ingredients to the dry and mix with a wooden spoon. Divide the cake batter equally among the lined cake pans. Tap the pans on the worktop a few times to remove any air bubbles.

5. Pop the cakes in the center of the oven and bake for around 30–35 minutes. You will know they are baked when they are springy to the touch and a knife or skewer inserted into the center of the cakes comes out clean. With colored cakes in particular, be very quick when opening the oven door to check them (if you leave the door open too long, the cakes can sink in the middle).

6. Once baked, place the cakes on a cooling rack and leave to cool fully, then pop them into a sealed container to keep them fresh before frosting.

Recipe continued on page 32

HOLLY'S TIP
Before frosting,
trim the cakes if needed
to make a flat surface—
don't discard these offcuts,
as you can crumble them
over the cake as
a decoration.

FROSTING

1. In a stand mixer, food processor, or using an electric hand mixer, cream the butter or margarine and cream cheese on high, then add in the confectioners' sugar and vanilla extract. Mix until the frosting is light and fluffy.

2. Fill and layer the cakes with the frosting (see page 211), then crumb-coat the whole cake (see page 212). As the frosting is quite soft, place the cake in the freezer for 15 minutes to firm up. This will make it easier to give it a final coat of frosting.

3. For the final coat, add a thick layer of frosting around the entire cake and smooth it out with a spatula or cake scraper. (See page 212 for how to apply the final coat.)

4. Put any leftover frosting into a piping bag fitted with an open star-tip nozzle and pipe swirls on the top of the cake.

This is best eaten within a few days of making. Store in a sealed container in the fridge. Leave the cake at room temperature for about 20 minutes before serving.

Classic Three-Tier Chocolate Celebration Cake

Who doesn't love a classic chocolate cake? I love to make three-tiered cakes, as they look more impressive—especially for an event—but you can make a two-tiered version if you want: just reduce the ingredients by a third. I've added some white chocolate curls to give this lush chocolate cake some contrast and extra presence.

Serves around 12

Cakes
- 2 cups (480 ml) dairy-free milk
- 2 teaspoons apple cider vinegar
- 3⅓ cups (420 g) self-rising flour
- 3 tablespoons cocoa powder
- 2⅓ cups (470 g) superfine sugar
- 1 teaspoon baking powder
- 1 teaspoon baking soda
- ½ cup (120 ml) sunflower oil

Chocolate buttercream
- 1¾ cups (400 g) dairy-free butter/margarine
- 5¾ cups (700 g) confectioners' sugar, sifted
- ¾ cup (120 g) cocoa powder

White chocolate curls
- 1 cup (170 g) dairy-free white chocolate, broken into chunks

CAKES

1. Preheat the oven to 400°F (200°C) and line three 8-inch (20 cm) round removable-bottom cake pans with parchment paper (see page 17 for how to line a cake pan). If you don't have three pans, you will have to bake the cakes separately. Keep the mixing bowl covered with a tea towel between bakes and stir the batter before use.

2. In a bowl, whisk the milk with the apple cider vinegar until fully combined. Set aside for 10 minutes to curdle—this creates a vegan buttermilk.

3. In a large mixing bowl, sift the flour, cocoa powder, superfine sugar, baking powder, and baking soda and mix well. Add the oil to the buttermilk and whisk to combine.

4. Add the wet ingredients to the dry and stir until fully mixed together. Divide the cake batter evenly among the lined cake pans. Tap the pans a few times on the worktop to remove any air bubbles.

5. Pop the cakes in the center of the oven and bake for around 28–30 minutes. You will know they are baked when they are springy to the touch and a knife or skewer inserted into the center of the cakes comes out clean.

6. Place the cakes on a cooling rack and allow to cool slightly before removing them from their pans (see page 17 for how to remove cakes from their pans). Return the cakes to the cooling rack. Once completely cool, pop them into a sealed container to keep them fresh until ready for frosting. This also softens the outside of the cakes.

Recipe continued on page 36

CHOCOLATE BUTTERCREAM

1. In a stand mixer, food processor, or using an electric hand mixer, cream the butter or margarine on high, then add the confectioners' sugar and cocoa powder.

2. Fill and stack the cakes with ⅓ of the buttercream (see page 211). You will need the rest for the crumb coat and final coat. Crumb-coat the cake (see page 212) and pop it into the fridge for about an hour to firm up before adding a final buttercream coating (see page 212).

3. Once set, apply the buttercream all over the cake with a palette knife, making large swirling patterns.

WHITE CHOCOLATE CURLS

1. Place a large baking sheet upside down on a kitchen worktop.

2. Temper the chocolate according to the instructions on page 207.

3. Once the chocolate is tempered, you will need to work quickly. Pour the chocolate onto the back of the baking sheet and spread it out using a large palette knife or an offset spatula. Let it cool slightly, but before it hardens fully, use a straight-edged metal spatula (I like to use a large putty knife) to push the chocolate at an angle to create the curls.

4. Place the curls to one side to harden fully before using them to decorate the cake.

This is best eaten within a few days of making. Store in a sealed container in or out of the fridge. If stored in the fridge, leave the cake at room temperature for about 20 minutes before serving.

HOLLY'S TIP

If the chocolate begins to harden too quickly after tempering, heat it for a few seconds with a hair dryer before making the curls.

Speculoos Cake

My speculoos recipes are always extremely popular on my blog and Instagram, and, because I favor the Biscoff brand, some of my followers have even dubbed me the Biscoff Queen—a title I'm very happy to accept (as long as it comes with a Biscoff cookie crown to match!).

Speculoos are a type of Belgian spiced cookie, traditionally eaten around Christmastime, but thankfully their huge popularity means these caramel-flavored cookies are now enjoyed all year-round. In fact, the delicious flavor is so popular you can even buy speculoos spreads, which make the ideal baking ingredient. This cake is oozing with speculoos flavor, from the moist sponge to the creamy frosting—plus it looks elegant and is definitely a crowd-pleaser! *See photo on page 40.*

Serves 18–20

Cakes
- 2 cups (480 ml) dairy-free milk
- 2 teaspoons apple cider vinegar
- 3⅓ cups (420 g) self-rising flour
- 2⅓ cups (470 g) superfine sugar
- 1 teaspoon baking powder
- 1 teaspoon baking soda
- 15 vegan speculoos cookies, ground (I use Biscoff)
- ½ cup (120 ml) sunflower oil

Buttercream
- 1½ cups (350 g) dairy-free block butter (not margarine)
- 6⅔ cups (800 g) confectioners' sugar, sifted
- ½ teaspoon vanilla extract
- Dash of dairy-free milk, if needed
- 9 tablespoons smooth vegan speculoos spread
- Around 8 vegan speculoos cookies, to decorate

CAKES

1. Preheat the oven to 400°F (200°C) and line three 8-inch (20 cm) round removable-bottom cake pans with parchment paper (see page 17 for how to line a cake pan). If you don't have three pans, you will have to bake them separately—keep the mixing bowl covered with a tea towel between bakes and stir the batter before use.

2. In a bowl, whisk the milk with the apple cider vinegar until fully combined. Set aside for 10 minutes to curdle—this creates a vegan buttermilk.

3. In a large bowl, sift the flour, superfine sugar, baking powder, and baking soda and mix well to combine. Stir in the ground cookies.

4. Add the oil to the buttermilk and whisk to combine, then add the wet ingredients to the dry and mix.

5. Divide the cake batter evenly among the lined cake pans. Tap the pans on the worktop a few times to remove any air bubbles.

6. Pop the cakes in the center of the oven and bake for around 35–40 minutes. You will know they are baked when they are springy to the touch and a knife or skewer inserted into the center of the cakes comes out clean.

7. Place the cakes on a cooling rack and allow them to cool slightly before removing them from the pans (see page 17 for how to remove a cake from its pan). Once cool, pop the cakes into a sealed container to keep them fresh until ready for frosting. This also softens the outside of the cakes.

BUTTERCREAM

1. Using an electric hand mixer or a stand mixer with a balloon-whisk attachment, cream the butter on high until smooth and creamy. Add the confectioners' sugar and vanilla extract. Whisk until the buttercream is light and fluffy. You can do this by hand, but it will take you longer. If the buttercream is too thick, add a dash of milk; if it's too wet, add more confectioners' sugar.

2. Place one of the cake layers on a cake turntable, serving plate, or cake board. Put a quarter of the buttercream into a piping bag fitted with a large round-tip nozzle. Pipe a ring of buttercream around the outer edge of the cake, then add around 3 tablespoons of speculoos spread to the center and spread it out toward the ring of buttercream using an offset spatula or knife. Lay the next cake layer on top and repeat. Place the final cake layer on top. (To get a level top layer and flat surface on your cake, see page 16.)

3. Using another quarter of the buttercream, crumb-coat the whole cake (see page 212) and pop it into the freezer for 15 minutes, or the fridge for around 30 minutes, to firm up.

4. Once firm, take the third quarter of the buttercream and add a thicker layer to the whole cake using a palette knife. Smooth out the buttercream on the sides and top of the cake using a cake scraper or palette knife (see page 212 for how to apply the final coat).

5. Melt the remaining speculoos spread, either in the microwave or in a small saucepan over low heat. Add it to a piping bag fitted with a small round-tip nozzle. If you don't have a nozzle, snip the end off a disposable piping bag. Pipe the melted spread around the top edge of the cake, encouraging it to slowly drip down the sides, then spread some to cover the top of the cake using an offset spatula or knife.

6. Add the remaining buttercream to a piping bag fitted with an open star-tip nozzle and pipe swirls around the top edge of the cake. Decorate with whole and crushed cookies.

This is best enjoyed within a few days of making. Store in a sealed container in the fridge and leave at room temperature for 20 minutes before serving.

Neapolitan Celebration Cake

My Neapolitan cake brings together three classic ice cream flavors into one impressive-looking cake. Indulge in tasty layers of chocolate, vanilla, and strawberry, topped off with a buttercream "ice cream" that will fool anyone into thinking it's real! Enjoy my showstopping spin on this summer celebration cake. *See photo on page 41.*

Serves around 12

Cakes
- 2 cups (480 ml) dairy-free milk
- 2 teaspoons apple cider vinegar
- 3⅓ cups (420 g) self-rising flour
- 2⅓ cups (470 g) superfine sugar
- 1 teaspoon baking powder
- 1 teaspoon baking soda
- ½ cup (120 ml) sunflower oil
- 1 teaspoon strawberry flavoring
- A few drops of pink gel food coloring
- 2 tablespoons cocoa powder
- 1 teaspoon vanilla extract

Buttercream
- 1½ cups plus 1 tablespoon (360 g) dairy-free butter/margarine
- 7 cups plus 2 tablespoons (860 g) confectioners' sugar, sifted
- ¼ teaspoon strawberry flavoring
- A few drops of pink gel food coloring
- 3 tablespoons cocoa powder
- ¼ teaspoon vanilla extract

- Waffle cone and vegan chocolate sauce, to decorate

CAKES

1. Preheat the oven to 400°F (200°C) and line three 6-inch (15 cm) round removable-bottom cake pans with parchment paper (see page 17 for how to line a cake pan). If you don't have three pans, you will have to bake the cakes separately. Keep the mixing bowl covered with a tea towel between bakes and stir the batter before use.

2. In a bowl, whisk the milk and the apple cider vinegar until fully combined. Set aside for 10 minutes to curdle—this creates a vegan buttermilk.

3. In a large mixing bowl, sift the flour, superfine sugar, baking powder, and baking soda. Mix well to combine. Add the oil to the buttermilk and whisk to combine.

4. Add the wet ingredients to the dry and mix. Divide the cake batter equally among three separate bowls.

5. To one bowl, add the strawberry flavoring and a few drops of pink gel food coloring, and mix until fully incorporated. To the second, add the cocoa powder and mix until fully combined. Add the vanilla extract to the final bowl and stir in.

6. Pour each of the batches of cake batter into a different pan. Place them in the center of the oven and bake for 28–30 minutes, or until the cakes are springy to the touch and a skewer or knife inserted into the center comes out clean.

7. Place the cakes on a cooling rack and allow to cool slightly before removing them from the pans (see page 17 for a tip on how to do this). Put the cakes on the rack to cool fully. Once cool, pop them into a sealed container to keep them fresh until ready for frosting. This also softens the outside of the cakes.

BUTTERCREAM

1. In a stand mixer, food processor, or using an electric hand mixer, cream the butter or margarine on high, then add the confectioners' sugar. Whip until creamy and fully combined. Divide the buttercream into three separate bowls.

2. To one bowl, add the strawberry flavoring and a few drops of pink gel food coloring and stir. To the second bowl, add the cocoa powder. Mix until fully incorporated. To the third bowl, add the vanilla extract and stir to combine.

3. Place the chocolate cake on a cake turntable, serving plate, or cake board and spread about 4 heaped tablespoons of the chocolate buttercream on top. Then lay the strawberry cake on top of the chocolate buttercream and spread about the same amount of the strawberry buttercream on top of this cake. Finally, lay the vanilla cake on top of the strawberry buttercream.

4. Crumb-coat the whole cake with the vanilla buttercream (see page 212). Remember to discard any of the buttercream scraped off, as it may have crumbs in it. Pop the cake into the fridge for about an hour to firm up.

5. Set aside an ice cream scoop's worth of each buttercream flavor for the ice cream decoration. Place these into the fridge to firm up. Once the crumb coat has set, use a palette knife to coat the bottom third of the cake with the remaining chocolate buttercream, the middle third with the remaining strawberry buttercream, and the top third with the vanilla buttercream. Spread some vanilla buttercream over the top of the cake and smooth out.

6. Use a cake scraper or palette knife to scrape around the cake, creating a smooth ombre effect. You may need to wipe the knife/scraper after each use so it doesn't affect the colors too much.

7. Remove the reserved buttercream from the fridge. Using an ice cream scoop, place 3 dollops on top of the cake (to resemble ice cream) and finish with an ice cream waffle cone. Drizzle chocolate sauce over the ice cream scoops and down the side of the cake.

This is best eaten within a few days of making. Store in a sealed container in or out of the fridge. If refrigerated, leave the cake at room temperature for about 20 minutes before serving.

Gingerbread Loaf Cake

A true classic served with a pinch of festive nostalgia. This is also one of my mom's favorite cakes, which she describes as a subtly spiced sponge complemented by a mildly sweet, creamy topping. You could turn this into a dessert by leaving off the cream cheese topping and serving a slice with dairy-free custard or ice cream.

Serves 8–10

Loaf
- 1½ cups plus 1½ table-spoons (200 g) self-rising flour
- ⅓ cup (60 g) superfine sugar
- ⅓ cup (60 g) dark brown sugar
- ½ teaspoon baking powder
- ¼ teaspoon baking soda
- 3 teaspoons ground ginger
- ½ teaspoon ground cinnamon
- ½ teaspoon ground nutmeg
- ½ cup (120 ml) dairy-free milk
- ¼ cup (60 ml) sunflower oil
- 3 tablespoons orange juice
- 1 tablespoon golden syrup
- 1 teaspoon vanilla extract

Frosting
- 2½ tablespoons dairy-free butter/margarine
- 2½ tablespoons dairy-free cream cheese
- 1⅔ cups (200 g) confectioners' sugar
- ¼ teaspoon vanilla extract

- Chopped or flaked almonds, for topping (optional)

LOAF

1. Preheat the oven to 400°F (200°C) and line a 9-by-5-inch (23 by 13 cm) loaf pan with parchment paper (see page 17 for how to line a loaf pan). Allow the paper to hang on either side of the pan so it makes it easier to remove the loaf when baked. In a large bowl, stir together the flour, sugars, baking powder, baking soda, ginger, cinnamon, and nutmeg and mix to break up any lumps.

2. In a separate bowl, mix the milk, oil, orange juice, golden syrup, and vanilla extract, whisking thoroughly to combine. Add the dry mixture to the wet and fold together until smooth and fully incorporated—don't overmix!

3. Pour the cake batter into the lined pan. Place in the middle of the oven and bake for 30–35 minutes, or until a skewer inserted into the center comes out clean.

4. Once baked, remove from the oven and allow to cool slightly before lifting out of the pan. Place on a cooling rack with the parchment paper. Allow to cool fully before frosting.

FROSTING

1. In a stand mixer with a balloon-whisk attachment, beat the butter or margarine, cream cheese, confectioners' sugar, and vanilla extract on high until smooth. You can use an electric hand mixer or a wooden spoon instead, but it will take longer.

2. When the loaf is cool, remove the parchment paper and place on a serving dish/plate. Smooth the frosting over the top. Decorate with the almonds, if using.

This is best eaten within a few days of making. Store in a sealed container in the fridge. Leave at room temperature for 15–20 minutes before serving.

Pineapple Upside-Down Cake

Upside-down cakes are a retro favorite! My version blends tropical coconut, juicy pineapple (I use canned), and sweet cherries to create a moist and fruity flavor sensation. Serve with dairy-free ice cream, a drizzle of dairy-free vanilla custard, or have it plain—either way, you'll be going back for second helpings!

Serves around 5–8

Cake

- 6 pineapple rings (from a can)
- 6 glacé cherries
- 1¼ cups (160 g) self-rising flour
- ½ cup (50 g) ground almonds
- ⅔ cup (50 g) shredded coconut
- 3 tablespoons superfine sugar
- 1 teaspoon baking powder
- ½ teaspoon baking soda
- ⅓ cup (90 ml) pineapple juice (from the can of pineapple rings)
- ¼ cup (80 g) maple syrup
- ½ cup (120 ml) dairy-free milk
- 2 tablespoons coconut oil, melted
- 2 teaspoons apple cider vinegar

1. Preheat the oven to 400°F (200°C) and line an 8-inch (20 cm) or 9-inch (23 cm) round removable-bottom cake pan with parchment paper (see page 17 for how to line a cake pan).

2. Arrange 6 pineapple rings in the base of the pan—you may need to trim the center ring to fit (or you can just use 5 rings). Place a glacé cherry in the center of each ring. Set aside.

3. Add the flour, ground almonds, shredded coconut, superfine sugar, baking powder, and baking soda to a mixing bowl. Stir well to combine.

4. In a separate bowl, whisk together the pineapple juice, maple syrup, milk, melted coconut oil, and apple cider vinegar until combined.

5. Pour the wet mixture into the dry and fold together with a spatula until fully combined.

6. Pour the cake batter over the pineapple rings in the pan. Tap to level the batter and release any air bubbles. Bake for 35–40 minutes, or until the sponge is springy to the touch and a skewer or knife inserted into the center comes out clean.

7. Remove from the oven and place on a cooling rack. Let the cake cool slightly before removing it from the pan. You will need to turn it upside down to remove it and serve. I do this by placing a serving plate on top of the cake and flipping it over. Serve warm with a scoop of ice cream or custard.

Best enjoyed on the day you make it, or you can also save it for later! Once cool, store in a sealed container in the fridge for 2 days. Leave at room temperature for 15–20 minutes before serving.

Double-Chocolate Banana Bread

Bananas and chocolate are like milk and cookies—they're so much better when they're together. This double-chocolate banana bread is loaded with sweet bananas, which are contrasted with bitter dark chocolate. Go all out and top it with some super-creamy chocolate ganache. You can save some in the fridge and warm it up when desired for the ultimate double-chocolate banana bread experience.

Serves 8–10

Loaf
- 4 ripe medium bananas (350 g)
- ⅓ cup plus ½ tablespoon (70 g) superfine sugar
- ¾ cup plus 1 tablespoon (200 ml) dairy-free milk
- 2½ cups plus 1 tablespoon (320 g) self-rising flour
- 5 tablespoons cocoa powder
- ¼ cup (40 g) dairy-free dark chocolate chips

Ganache (optional)
- ¾ cup plus 2 tablespoons (150 g) dairy-free dark chocolate chips
- ¼ cup (50 g) dairy-free cream

LOAF

1. Preheat the oven to 375°F (190°C) and line a 9-by-5-inch (23 by 13 cm) loaf pan with parchment paper (see page 17 for how to line a loaf pan). Allow the paper to hang on either side of the pan to make it easier to remove the loaf when baked.

2. Peel and roughly chop the bananas and place them in a medium bowl. Mash the bananas with a fork or potato masher. Add the superfine sugar and milk and stir with a wooden spoon to combine. Add the flour and cocoa powder and fold until fully combined, then fold in the chocolate chips.

3. Pour the banana bread mixture into the lined pan. As the mixture is quite thick, use a small spatula or spoon to smooth it into the corners of the pan.

4. Place the pan in the middle of the oven and bake for 65–70 minutes. After 45 minutes, place some foil on top of the banana bread to prevent it from burning. Once baked, remove from the oven and allow to cool slightly before lifting the loaf out of the pan. Place on a cooling rack and allow to cool fully before removing the parchment paper and adding the ganache, if using.

GANACHE

1. Place the chocolate and cream in a medium saucepan over medium heat and simmer, stirring continuously, until the chocolate has melted and is glossy.

2. Spread the ganache over the top of the banana bread and smooth out with the back of a spoon or a small spatula. When the ganache cools, it will thicken up. Use a serrated knife to slice the banana bread into servings.

Best enjoyed on the day you make it, but it will keep in a sealed container in the fridge for 2–3 days. Leave at room temperature for 15 minutes before serving.

Chocolate Lava Cakes

My chocolate lava cakes are the definition of melt-in-your-mouth deliciousness, with their rich chocolate sponge and gooey molten cores. My recipe is fairly easy to make, and I'm sure you'll absolutely "lava" the mouthwatering result! You could enjoy these as a festive dessert and set them alight with some vegan-friendly brandy, then serve them with your favorite dairy-free cream, ice cream, or fresh berries. These are great to serve a crowd: simply double the recipe if you've got more people to feed.

Serves 3

Cakes
- Coconut oil, melted, for greasing
- ¾ cup plus 3⅓ tablespoons (120 g) all-purpose flour
- ¾ cup plus 2½ tablespoons (110 g) confectioners' sugar, sifted
- ¼ cup (30 g) cocoa powder, plus extra to decorate
- ½ tablespoon instant ground coffee
- ½ teaspoon baking powder
- ½ teaspoon baking soda
- 1 small ripe banana
- ½ cup (120 ml) dairy-free milk
- ½ tablespoon apple cider vinegar
- ½ tablespoon vanilla bean paste

Chocolate filling
- ¾ cup (120 g) dairy-free chocolate, broken into chunks

HOLLY'S TIP

If the cakes cool too much before serving, revive them by briefly warming them in the oven or microwave.

CAKES

1. Preheat the oven to 400°F (200°C). Grease three individual 4-by-2-inch (10 by 7½ cm) ramekins with coconut oil.

2. Sift the flour, confectioners' sugar, cocoa powder, coffee, baking powder, and baking soda into a medium bowl and mix to combine.

3. In a separate bowl, mash the banana, then add the milk, apple cider vinegar, and vanilla bean paste. Whisk to combine.

4. Add the wet ingredients to the dry and fold together—don't overmix! Divide half of the batter among the ramekins, then carefully press a third of the chocolate chunks into the center of each ramekin. Spoon the remaining batter over the chocolate chunks until they are completely hidden. You don't want to overfill them, as the sponge will rise in the ramekins.

5. Place the ramekins on a baking sheet and place the sheet in the center of the oven. Bake for 20–25 minutes. Once baked, carefully run a knife around the edge of each ramekin to help loosen the sponge.

6. Place a plate on top of each ramekin in turn, flip upside down, then lift off the ramekin. Serve the cakes with a dusting of cocoa powder, along with dairy-free cream, ice cream, and fresh berries (optional).

The chocolate will be runny while the sponge is hot but will become less so as it cools, so these are best enjoyed straight from the oven.

Mocha Swiss Roll

Mocha is a delicious blend of espresso, milk, and chocolate. My Swiss roll takes the mocha flavor to the next level, with a coffee-infused chocolate sponge and velvety ganache. For those of you who aren't as coffee-obsessed as I am, you can leave the coffee out for a delicious chocolate Swiss roll.

Serves 8–10

Sponge
- ¾ cup plus 1 tablespoon (200 ml) dairy-free milk
- 1 teaspoon apple cider vinegar
- 1⅔ cups (200 g) all-purpose flour
- ½ cup (100 g) superfine sugar
- 2 tablespoons cocoa powder, plus extra for rolling the cake
- 1 tablespoon ground instant coffee
- 4 tablespoons cornstarch
- ½ teaspoon baking soda
- ½ teaspoon baking powder
- ⅓ cup (80 ml) aquafaba
- 3½ tablespoons (50 ml) sunflower oil

Filling
- ⅓ cup plus 1½ tablespoons (100 g) dairy-free butter/margarine
- 2 cups plus 1 tablespoon (250 g) confectioners' sugar, sifted
- 1 teaspoon vanilla extract
- 1 tablespoon dairy-free cream

Ingredients continued on page 54

SPONGE

1. Preheat the oven to 400°F (200°C) and fully line a 15-by-10-inch (38 by 25 cm) rectangular baking sheet with parchment paper (see page 17 for how to line a baking sheet).

2. In a bowl, whisk together the milk and apple cider vinegar and set aside for 10 minutes—this creates a vegan buttermilk. In a separate bowl, mix together the flour, superfine sugar, cocoa powder, coffee, cornstarch, baking soda, and baking powder.

3. Add the aquafaba and oil to the vegan buttermilk and stir to combine. Pour the wet mixture into the dry and stir with a wooden spoon until just incorporated.

4. Pour the cake batter onto the lined baking sheet and use a spoon or spatula to spread it evenly into the corners. Tap the sheet on the worktop a few times to remove any air bubbles.

5. Bake for 20 minutes or until it is springy to the touch and a skewer inserted into the center comes out clean (don't overbake, or it will dry out and crack when you roll it).

6. Remove from the oven and place the baking sheet on a wire rack to cool only slightly, as it still needs to be warm to roll it. Lay a large piece of parchment paper on top of a clean tea towel on the worktop and sprinkle over some cocoa powder.

7. You may need to run a knife around the edges of the sheet to loosen the sponge. Then, invert the sponge onto the parchment paper and tea towel. You can now carefully peel off the parchment paper from the sponge.

Recipe continued on page 54

Ganache

- 1 cup plus 1 tablespoon (180 g) dairy-free chocolate, broken up
- 1 tablespoon instant coffee
- ¼ cup (50 g) dairy-free cream
- Swirls of whipped cream (optional), a sprinkle of cocoa powder, and instant coffee, to decorate

HOLLY'S TIP

If your kitchen feels warm, pop the filling in the fridge for 10 minutes to set slightly before using.

8. Trim the edges of the sponge with a sharp serrated knife—this will give the sponge a better shape and make it easier to roll. From one of the shorter sides, roll up the sponge with the parchment paper and tea towel inside, making sure to roll it tightly at the start. Rolling the sponge up with the parchment paper inside helps it to keep its shape and prevents it from sticking. Set aside to cool completely.

FILLING

1. In a stand mixer, cream the butter or margarine on high, then add the confectioners' sugar, vanilla extract, and cream (you can use a wooden spoon, but it will take longer). Add more confectioners' sugar if the consistency is too soft.

2. Carefully unroll the sponge and spread a thin layer of the filling on it. Reroll it tightly but this time without the tea towel and parchment paper inside. You may get some cracks in the Swiss roll as you reroll it: this is normal and they will be covered by the ganache. Pop the Swiss roll into the freezer while you make the ganache.

GANACHE

1. Place the chocolate, coffee, and cream into a medium saucepan over medium heat and simmer, stirring continuously, until it has melted and is glossy. You can use the ganache right away or allow it to cool down for a thicker consistency.

2. Carefully transfer the Swiss roll to a serving plate or baking sheet. Using an offset spatula or knife, spread the ganache all over it. As the Swiss roll has been chilled, it will set the ganache as you spread it. Transfer it back to the freezer for about 5 minutes to set the ganache further.

3. Trim both ends of the Swiss roll to reveal the swirl (you can eat the ends—they're just as delicious!). Decorate with swirls of whipped cream, if using, a dusting of cocoa powder, and a sprinkling of coffee.

This is best enjoyed on the day you make it, but you can store it in the fridge in a sealed container for a few days. Leave at room temperature for around 20 minutes before serving.

Winter Wonderland Orange and Cinnamon Cake

The holiday season is a very special time for me, and I will always treasure the time I got to spend with my adorable cat, Tiggs. I would curl up on the sofa with a blanket and a bowl of salted popcorn to watch our favorite movie, *How the Grinch Stole Christmas*, and Tiggs would be fast asleep beside me. This movie holds a special place in my heart and inspired the gingerbread cookie houses you see on my festive cake. The houses remind me of the fictional town of Whoville, with their crisp layer of white snowy frosting and whimsically decorated exteriors.

The cake itself is a moist orange and cinnamon sponge with a light, velvety orange-flavored cream cheese frosting. It makes the perfect centerpiece for any festive occasion and will put a huge smile on everyone's face. I want to dedicate this festive bake to my special boy and best friend: my cat, Tiggs. *See photo on page 57.*

Serves 18–20

Gingerbread cookies
- 1 batch of gingerbread cookies (see page 147)

Royal icing
- ½ batch of royal icing (see page 200)

Cakes
- 2 cups (480 ml) dairy-free milk
- 2 teaspoons apple cider vinegar
- 3⅓ cups (420 g) self-rising flour
- 2 cups plus 1 tablespoon (420 g) superfine sugar
- 2½ teaspoons ground cinnamon
- 1 teaspoon baking powder
- 1 teaspoon baking soda
- ½ cup (120 ml) sunflower oil
- 2½ teaspoons orange extract or flavoring

Ingredients continued on page 56

GINGERBREAD HOUSES/CHARACTERS

1. Follow the recipe for gingerbread cookies on page 147, making them in advance and allowing time for the icing to set. Make the gingerbread houses, trees, snowflakes, and bear using various cookie cutters—I made 8 houses, 5 trees, 1 bear, and several snowflakes. If you don't have the exact shapes, get creative with any festive cookie cutters you do have. If you don't have any cookie cutters at all, you can print out templates from the internet and use a knife to cut them out.

2. Decorate the cookies using royal icing. See pages 208–210 for tips on this.

CAKES

1. Preheat the oven to 400°F (200°C) and line three 8-inch (20 cm) round removable-bottom cake pans with parchment paper. If you only have one pan, you will have to bake the cakes separately. Keep the mixing bowl covered with a tea towel between bakes and stir the batter before use.

2. In a bowl, whisk the milk with the apple cider vinegar until fully combined. Set aside for 10 minutes to curdle—this creates a vegan buttermilk.

3. In a large mixing bowl, sift the flour, superfine sugar, ground cinnamon, baking powder, and baking soda. Mix with a wooden spoon to combine.

Recipe continued on page 56

Frosting
- 1⅓ cups (300 g) dairy-free butter/margarine
- 2 tablespoons dairy-free cream cheese
- ½ teaspoon orange extract or flavoring
- 5⅓ cups (650 g) confectioners' sugar, sifted
- Dash of dairy-free milk, if needed
- ¼ cup (20 g) shredded coconut and a dusting of confectioners' sugar, to decorate

4. Add the oil and orange extract or flavoring to the buttermilk and whisk to combine, then add the wet ingredients to the dry and mix.

5. Divide the cake batter equally among the lined cake pans. Make sure to tap the pans on the worktop a few times to remove any air bubbles.

6. Pop the cakes into the center of the oven and bake for around 28–30 minutes. You will know they are baked when they are springy to the touch and a knife or skewer inserted into the center of the cake comes out clean.

7. Place the cakes on a cooling rack and allow them to cool slightly before removing them from the pans (see page 17 for how to remove cakes from their pans). Put the cakes on the rack to cool fully. Once cool, pop them into a sealed container to keep them fresh until ready for frosting.

FROSTING

1. In a stand mixer, cream the butter or margarine and the cream cheese together on high speed until smooth and creamy, then add the orange extract or flavoring and the confectioners' sugar. Whisk until the frosting is light and fluffy. You can do this by hand, but it will take you longer. If the frosting is too thick, add a dash of milk; if it's too wet, add more confectioners' sugar. The frosting is needed for filling the cake, the crumb coat, the final coat, the decoration on the top of the cake, and sticking the gingerbread cookies onto the cake.

2. Place one of the cake layers on a cake turntable, serving plate, or cake board. Frost the top, then place the second cake layer on top and repeat until all three layers are sandwiched together with frosting.

3. Using a palette knife, crumb-coat the whole cake (see page 212). Place the cake in the freezer for 15 minutes or in the fridge for 30 minutes to firm up. This will make it easier to apply the final coat of frosting.

4. Once firm, add a thicker layer of frosting to the whole cake using a palette knife. Smooth out the frosting on the sides and top of the cake using a cake scraper or a palette knife (see page 212 for how to apply the final coat).

5. Add some of the leftover frosting to a piping bag fitted with a pastry nozzle and pipe a decorative border along the top outer edge of the cake. If you don't have a pastry nozzle, use any decorative nozzle you have.

HOLLY'S TIP

To get even cake
layers, weigh out the
cake batter before pouring
it into the cake pans.

6. Press shredded coconut all over the cake to resemble snow.

7. Use some leftover frosting to stick the iced gingerbread houses, trees, etc. around the sides of the cake. Place a toothpick behind the trees and characters for the top of the cake and secure with some frosting. Stick them into the top of the cake. (The toothpicks will keep them upright and in place, but remember to remove the toothpicks before serving.) Decorate with some shredded coconut and sifted confectioners' sugar to resemble snow.

This is best eaten within a few days. Store in a sealed container in the fridge and leave at room temperature for 20 minutes before serving.

Chocolate or Vanilla Cupcakes

This recipe can be used to make either chocolate or vanilla cupcakes: simply use cocoa powder or vanilla extract in the mixture, depending on which you're making. These cupcakes are light and fluffy with a soft, sweet topping, ideal for any occasion. Swiss meringue buttercream (page 198) would also be delicious here. You can top them with colorful sprinkles, fruit, or dairy-free chocolate drops or shavings to add texture and wow factor—or they taste delicious on their own. Happiness is only a cupcake away!

Makes 8–10 cupcakes

Cupcakes
- 1 cup (240 ml) dairy-free milk
- 1 teaspoon apple cider vinegar
- 1⅔ cups (210 g) self-rising flour
- ½ cup (100 g) superfine sugar
- ½ teaspoon baking powder
- ½ teaspoon baking soda
- 3 tablespoons cocoa powder (for chocolate cupcakes) or 1 teaspoon vanilla extract (for vanilla cupcakes)
- ¼ cup (60 ml) sunflower oil

Chocolate buttercream
- ½ cup (120 g) dairy-free butter/margarine
- 3⅓ cups (400 g) confectioners' sugar, sifted
- 3 tablespoons cocoa powder
- Dash of dairy-free milk, if needed

Vanilla buttercream
- ½ cup (120 g) dairy-free butter/margarine
- 3⅓ cups (400 g) confectioners' sugar, sifted
- 1 teaspoon vanilla extract
- Dash of dairy-free milk, if needed

CUPCAKES

1. Preheat the oven to 400°F (200°C) and line two cupcake pans with cupcake liners. In a small bowl, whisk the milk with the apple cider vinegar until fully combined. Set aside for 10 minutes to curdle—this creates a vegan buttermilk.

2. In a large mixing bowl, sift the flour, superfine sugar, baking powder, baking soda, and cocoa, if making chocolate cupcakes. Mix well to combine.

3. Add the oil to the buttermilk and whisk to combine. If you're making vanilla cupcakes, add the vanilla extract and combine. Add the wet ingredients to the dry and mix until smooth.

4. Fill the liners three-quarters full with the batter. Make sure to tap the pan on the worktop a few times to remove any air bubbles. Pop the cakes into the center of the oven and bake for 18–20 minutes. You will know the cakes are done when they are springy to the touch and a knife or skewer inserted into the center comes out clean.

5. Place the cupcakes on a cooling rack and allow to cool fully before frosting.

BUTTERCREAM

1. Check the ingredients closely, as quantities differ between the chocolate and the vanilla buttercream, but the method stays the same. In a stand mixer, cream the butter or margarine on high using a balloon-whisk attachment. You can use a wooden spoon, but it will take longer.

2. When your butter or margarine is creamy and light in color, add the confectioners' sugar and cocoa powder or vanilla extract (depending on which cupcake you are making). Whizz together until fluffy and fully combined. Add a dash of dairy-free milk if the mixture is too thick.

3. Transfer the buttercream to a piping bag fitted with an open star-tip nozzle. Core the cupcakes halfway down with an apple corer and fill with the buttercream. Then pipe a swirl of buttercream on top of each cupcake.

Serve these cupcakes fresh or store in a sealed container in or out of the fridge. The buttercream will firm up at room temperature. Best eaten within a few days of making.

Black Forest Cupcakes

Black Forest cake is named after the area in Germany where kirsch (cherry liquor), a key ingredient, originated. German law mandates that any dessert labeled "Black Forest cake" must contain kirsch. My vegan Black Forest–inspired cupcakes feature dark chocolate with rich cherry undertones. You can go all out and add a few teaspoons of kirsch to the cherry sauce. *See photo on page 62.*

Makes 8–10 cupcakes

Cherry sauce
- ⅔ cup (150 g) cherries, pitted and chopped
- ⅓ cup (60 g) superfine sugar
- 1 tablespoon cornstarch
- 1 tablespoon lemon juice
- 2 teaspoons vegan-friendly cherry liqueur (optional)

Cupcakes
- 1 cup (240 ml) dairy-free milk
- 1 teaspoon apple cider vinegar
- 1⅔ cups (210 g) self-rising flour
- 3 tablespoons cocoa powder
- ⅓ cup plus 1 tablespoon (80 g) superfine sugar
- ½ teaspoon baking powder
- ½ teaspoon baking soda
- ¼ cup (60 ml) sunflower oil

Frosting
- ⅓ cup plus 1 tablespoon (100 g) dairy-free butter/margarine
- 1¼ tablespoons dairy-free cream cheese
- ¼ cup (30 g) cocoa powder
- 1¾ cup (210 g) confectioners' sugar, sifted
- 2 teaspoons vegan-friendly cherry liqueur (optional)
- Dash of dairy-free milk, if needed
- Dairy-free white chocolate shavings and fresh cherries, to decorate (optional)

CHERRY SAUCE

1. Place the pitted and chopped cherries in a medium saucepan and sprinkle over the superfine sugar, cornstarch, and lemon juice. Place over medium heat and bring to a boil. If the cherries are too big, you can use a fork or potato masher to crush them.

2. Simmer for 6–8 minutes, stirring occasionally with a wooden spoon or heatproof spatula, until thickened. Remove from the heat and add the cherry liqueur, if using. Alcohol evaporates when cooked, so it's best to add it at the end. Allow to cool fully before filling the cupcakes.

CUPCAKES

1. Preheat the oven to 400°F (200°C) and line two cupcake pans with cupcake liners. In a small bowl, whisk the milk with the apple cider vinegar until fully combined. Set aside for 10 minutes to curdle—this creates a vegan buttermilk.

2. In a large mixing bowl, sift the flour, cocoa powder, superfine sugar, baking powder, and baking soda. Mix well to combine.

3. Add the oil to the buttermilk and whisk to combine. Pour the wet ingredients into the dry and mix with a wooden spoon until a smooth batter forms. Fill the liners three-quarters full with the batter. Tap the pans on the worktop a few times to remove any air bubbles.

4. Pop the pans into the oven and bake for 18–20 minutes. You will know the cakes are done when they are springy to the touch and a knife or skewer inserted into the center comes out clean. Place the cupcakes on a cooling rack and allow to cool fully before frosting. Store in a sealed container until you're ready to frost and decorate.

THE ESSENTIAL BOOK OF VEGAN BAKES

HOLLY'S TIP

Be careful
when serving fresh
cherries with the pits
inside. Let your guests
know that they will need
to pitted the cherry
before eating.

FROSTING

1. Whisk the butter or margarine and cream cheese in a bowl until creamy—I use my stand mixer with the balloon-whisk attachment on high speed. You can do it with an electric mixer, food processor, or by hand (but it will take longer by hand).

2. When your butter or margarine is creamy and light in color, add the cocoa powder and confectioners' sugar. Whizz together until fluffy and fully combined.

3. Add in the cherry liquor, if using, and give a final mix until it's incorporated. If the frosting is too thick, you can add in a dash of dairy-free milk.

4. Core the cupcakes halfway down with an apple corer and fill with the cherry sauce. I use a piping bag for this, but you can use a small spoon.

5. Transfer the frosting to a piping bag fitted with an open star-tip nozzle. Pipe a swirl of frosting onto each cupcake. If you don't have a piping bag, you can simply spoon the frosting on top.

6. Decorate each cupcake with white chocolate shavings and a fresh cherry, if using (see Tip).

HOLLY'S TIP

Before frosting, you
can store the cupcakes in a
sealed container—this helps
to keep them moist and
makes it easier to remove
the liners.

Serve the cupcakes fresh or store in a sealed container in the fridge—the frosting will firm up at room temperature. If storing in the fridge, let rest at room temperature for 15 minutes before seving. Best eaten within a few days of making.

Cookies-and-Cream Cupcakes

Something magical happens when you crumble chocolate cookies into cake batter and buttercream: you create the most indulgent cupcakes, which are sure to delight. I've also included a cookie at the base of these cupcakes for an extra surprise! This is the perfect cupcake for parties and gatherings, or just to treat yourself with. *See photo on page 63.*

Makes around 12

Cupcakes
- 18 vegan chocolate cream cookies (I use Oreos)
- 1 cup (240 ml) dairy-free milk
- 1 teaspoon apple cider vinegar
- 1⅔ cups (210 g) self-rising flour
- 1 cup plus 2½ tablespoons (230 g) superfine sugar
- ½ teaspoon baking powder
- ½ teaspoon baking soda
- ¼ cup (60 ml) sunflower oil

Buttercream
- ⅔ cup (150 g) dairy-free butter/margarine
- 2½ cups (300 g) confectioners' sugar, sifted
- 1 teaspoon vanilla extract
- 8 vegan chocolate cream cookies (I use Oreos), finely crushed
- Dash of dairy-free milk, if needed

- 12 vegan chocolate cream cookies, for decoration (I use Oreos)

CUPCAKES

1. Preheat the oven to 400°F (200°C) and line two cupcake pans with cupcake liners. Add one whole cookie to the base of each cupcake liner.

2. In a small bowl, whisk the milk with the apple cider vinegar until fully combined. Set the mixture aside for 10 minutes to curdle—this creates a vegan buttermilk.

3. In a large mixing bowl, sift the flour, superfine sugar, baking powder, and baking soda. Mix well to combine. Add the oil to the buttermilk and whisk to combine.

4. Add the wet ingredients to the dry and mix until smooth. Chop the remaining 6 cookies into small, rough chunks and fold them into the batter. Don't overmix or it will turn gray—you want it to stay pale, with chunks of the cookies still visible.

5. Fill the liners three-quarters full with the cake batter. Tap the pans on the worktop a few times to remove any air bubbles.

6. Pop the cakes into the oven and bake for 18–20 minutes. You will know they are done when they are springy to the touch and a knife or skewer inserted into the center comes out clean. Place the cupcakes on a cooling rack and allow to cool fully before frosting. They can also be stored in a sealed container out of the fridge overnight before frosting.

BUTTERCREAM

1. Cream the butter or margarine until creamy. I use my stand mixer with the balloon-whisk attachment on high speed. You could use a hand mixer or a wooden spoon, but it will take longer. When your butter or margarine is creamy and light in color, add the confectioners' sugar, vanilla extract, and crushed cookies. Whizz together until fluffy and fully combined. Add a dash of milk if the mixture is too thick.

2. Transfer the buttercream to a piping bag fitted with a large round-tip nozzle. Pipe a blob of buttercream onto each cupcake and top with a whole cookie. Add the cookie just prior to serving to prevent it from softening.

Serve these cupcakes fresh or store in a sealed container in or out of the fridge—the buttercream will firm up at room temperature. Best eaten within a few days. If stored in the fridge, leave at room temperature for 15 minutes before serving.

Strawberry Cupcakes

These strawberry cupcakes are fresh, fruity, and look super-cute. Take a bite into the creamy frosting to reveal a jam-filled center (to make your own jam, see page 203). Top off with real strawberries to bring a sweet and juicy taste.

Makes 12 cupcakes

Cupcakes
- 1 cup (240 ml) dairy-free milk
- 1 teaspoon apple cider vinegar
- 1⅔ cups (210 g) self-rising flour
- ½ cup (100 g) superfine sugar
- ½ teaspoon baking powder
- ½ teaspoon baking soda
- ¼ cup (60 ml) sunflower oil
- ½ teaspoon strawberry flavoring
- 5 tablespoons (100 g) strawberry jam, for the filling

Buttercream
- ⅔ cup (150 g) dairy-free block butter (not margarine)
- 2½ cups (300 g) confectioners' sugar, sifted
- 1 teaspoon strawberry flavoring
- 4 tablespoons freeze-dried strawberries
- Drop of pink gel food coloring (optional)
- ¼ cup (50 ml) aquafaba

- Fresh strawberries, to decorate (optional)

CUPCAKES

1. Preheat the oven to 400°F (200°C) and line two cupcake pans with cupcake liners. In a small bowl, whisk the milk with the apple cider vinegar until fully combined. Set aside for 10 minutes to curdle—this creates a vegan buttermilk.

2. In a large mixing bowl, sift the flour, superfine sugar, baking powder, and baking soda. Mix well to combine.

3. Add the oil and the strawberry flavoring to the buttermilk and whisk to combine. Add the wet ingredients to the dry and mix until smooth.

4. Fill the cupcake liners three-quarters full with cake batter. Tap the pans on the worktop a few times to remove any air bubbles.

5. Pop the cakes into the center of the oven and bake for 18–20 minutes. You will know they are done when they are springy to the touch and a knife or skewer inserted into the center comes out clean. Place the cupcakes on a cooling rack and allow to cool fully before frosting.

BUTTERCREAM

1. Cream the butter. I use my stand mixer with the balloon-whisk attachment on high speed. You could use a hand mixer or a wooden spoon, but it will take longer.

2. When the butter is creamy and light in color, add the confectioners' sugar, strawberry flavoring, freeze-dried strawberries, and gel food coloring, if using, and combine. Then add the aquafaba and whizz on high speed for a few minutes until the buttercream is creamy and fluffy. If it is too thick, add a little more butter.

3. Core the cupcakes halfway down with an apple corer and fill with the jam. I use a piping bag for this, but you can use a small spoon.

4. Transfer the buttercream to a piping bag fitted with a large open star-tip nozzle. Pipe a swirl onto each cupcake and decorate with fresh strawberries, if using.

The buttercream will firm up. Serve fresh or store in a sealed container in the fridge for a few days. Leave at room temperature for 15 minutes before serving.

Pistachio and Coconut Cupcakes

Pistachios have a distinct, nutty flavor and taste even better when paired with sweet coconut in these lavish cupcakes. Pistachio is one of my favorite ice cream flavors, so I wanted to create a dessert featuring pistachio, and these cupcakes are perfection. If you want to dial up the color, you can add some green gel food coloring to make these a brighter shade of green.

Makes 8–10 cupcakes

Cupcakes
- 1 cup (240 ml) dairy-free milk
- 1 teaspoon apple cider vinegar
- Drop of green gel food coloring (optional)
- 1⅔ cups (210 g) self-rising flour
- ⅓ cup plus 1 tablespoon (80 g) superfine sugar
- ½ teaspoon baking powder
- ½ teaspoon baking soda
- ½ cup (60 g) shelled pistachios, chopped
- ¼ cup (60 ml) sunflower oil

Frosting
- ⅓ cup plus 1 tablespoon (90 g) dairy-free butter/margarine
- 1 tablespoon dairy-free cream cheese
- 2½ cups (300 g) confectioners' sugar, sifted
- 1 teaspoon vanilla extract
- Dash of dairy-free milk, if needed

- ⅔ cup (50 g) shredded coconut
- Whole pistachios, shelled, to decorate

CUPCAKES

1. Preheat the oven to 400°F (200°C) and line two cupcake pans with cupcake liners. In a small bowl, combine the milk, apple cider vinegar, and a small drop of green gel food coloring, if desired, and whisk until fully combined. Set aside for 10 minutes to curdle—this creates a vegan buttermilk.

2. In a large mixing bowl, sift the flour, superfine sugar, baking powder, and baking soda. Mix well to combine.

3. Place the pistachios in a food processor. Whizz until finely chopped, then add them to the flour mixture.

4. Add the oil to the buttermilk and whisk to combine. Add the wet ingredients to the dry and mix until smooth.

5. Fill the liners three-quarters full with the cake batter. Tap the pans a few times on the worktop to remove any air bubbles. Pop the cakes into the center of the oven and bake for 18–20 minutes. You will know they are done when they are springy to the touch and a knife or skewer inserted into the center comes out clean. Place the cupcakes on a cooling rack and cool fully before frosting.

FROSTING

1. Cream the butter or margarine and cream cheese until creamy. I use my stand mixer with the balloon-whisk attachment on high speed. You could use a hand mixer or a wooden spoon, but it will take longer.

2. When creamy and light in color, add the confectioners' sugar and vanilla extract. Whizz together until fluffy and fully combined. Add a dash of milk if the mixture is too thick.

HOLLY'S TIP

If you don't have
a round-tip nozzle, you can
use the piping bag without
a nozzle, or you could
simply spoon on
the frosting.

3. Transfer the frosting to a piping bag fitted with a round-tip nozzle. Pipe a swirl of frosting onto each cupcake.

4. Place the shredded coconut in a bowl and roll the top of the cupcakes in it. Top off with a few whole pistachios.

The frosting will firm up at room temperature. These are best eaten within a few days of making. Store in the fridge in a sealed container and leave them at room temperature for around 15 minutes before serving.

HOLLY'S TIP

Before frosting, you
can store the cupcakes in a
sealed container—this helps
to keep them moist and
makes it easier to remove
the liners.

Blueberry and Chia Muffins

My traditional blueberry muffins are juicy, sweet, and bursting with fresh blueberries. I've added chia seeds for added texture, antioxidants, and omega-3 fatty acids for a completely delicious variation.

Makes around 12 muffins

- 2 cups plus 1½ table-spoons (260 g) self-rising flour
- ¾ cup (150 g) superfine sugar
- 1 teaspoon baking powder
- ¼ teaspoon baking soda
- 1 tablespoon chia seeds
- 1 cup (240 ml) dairy-free milk
- ⅓ cup plus 1 tablespoon (100 g) dairy-free plain yogurt, plus extra to serve
- ¼ cup (60 ml) sunflower oil
- 1 teaspoon lemon juice
- 2 teaspoons vanilla extract
- 1¼ cups (150 g) fresh blueberries

- Blueberry compote/jam, to serve (optional; store-bought or see page 203 for my recipe)

1. Preheat the oven to 400°F (200°C) and line two muffin pans with muffin liners.

2. In a bowl, combine the flour, superfine sugar, baking powder, baking soda, and chia seeds.

3. In a separate bowl, combine the milk, yogurt, oil, lemon juice, and vanilla extract.

4. Pour the wet ingredients into the dry and mix until combined, but don't overmix! Fold in almost all of the blueberries (about 1 cup).

5. Fill the muffin liners three-quarters full with the batter. Scatter the remaining blueberries on top of the muffins and gently press down. Place in the center of the oven and bake for 15–20 minutes, or until a skewer inserted into the center comes out clean and the muffins are golden brown.

6. Once baked, place on a cooling rack and leave to cool. Once cool, store in a sealed container in the fridge.

Serve with extra yogurt, blueberry compote, or just as they are. Best enjoyed within a few days of making. Leave at room temperature for 15 minutes before serving.

DOUGHNUTS, PASTRIES, AND BUNS

Mixed Berry Parcels

They say the best things come in small packages, or in this case, parcels! These mini puff-pastry parcels are packed full of fruitiness and are delicious served fresh and warm, topped with a scoop of dairy-free ice cream. They also taste amazing chilled and drizzled with dairy-free custard. Ready-to-roll pastry makes this recipe super quick and easy, and it can also be made gluten-free if you use gluten-free ready-to-roll pastry.

Makes 8 parcels

Parcels
- 2½ cups (300 g) mixed berries (fresh or frozen)
- ½ cup (100 g) superfine sugar
- 1 teaspoon lemon juice
- 1 tablespoon cornstarch
- 2 sheets of ready-to-roll vegan puff pastry (gluten-free, if preferred)
- Flour, for dusting (gluten-free, if preferred)

Glaze
- 1 tablespoon dairy-free milk
- 1 tablespoon superfine sugar, to coat

1. Place the mixed berries in a medium saucepan and sprinkle over the superfine sugar, lemon juice, and cornstarch. Place over medium-high heat and bring to a boil. Simmer for 10–15 minutes until the mixture thickens, stirring occasionally with a wooden spoon or spatula to prevent it from burning. Once thickened, remove from the heat and allow to cool slightly (it will thicken further as it cools).

2. Preheat the oven to 400°F (200°C) and line two baking sheets with parchment paper (see page 17 for how to line a baking sheet). Unroll the puff pastry sheets onto a floured surface and cut each sheet into eight equal-sized rectangles.

3. Take two rectangles and spoon about 1 tablespoon of the berry mixture onto one of them. Sandwich the rectangles together. Repeat for the other parcels.

4. Transfer to the lined baking sheets and use a fork to press the edges of the parcels together to seal in the filling. Brush dairy-free milk over each parcel and sprinkle over some superfine sugar.

5. Place the baking sheets in the oven and bake for around 20 minutes, or until the pastry is crisp and golden brown. Allow to cool on a cooling rack.

Serve on the day you make them.

Cinnamon Rolls

Fluffy, sweet, and buttery with a cinnamon-spice flavor—in other words, the perfect cinnamon roll! These are the ultimate treat for cozying up next to a crackling log fire and sipping on a hot chocolate in the wintertime. Simple to make, drool-worthy to look at, and they won't last long on your plate. *See photos on pages 78–79.*

Makes 9–12

Rolls
- 1 cup (240 ml) dairy-free milk
- 2 tablespoons dairy-free butter/margarine
- 3½ teaspoons active dry yeast
- 1 tablespoon superfine sugar
- 3⅓ cups (410 g) self-rising flour, plus extra for kneading
- 3 teaspoons ground cinnamon
- Sunflower oil, for greasing the bowl

Filling
- 2 tablespoons dairy-free butter/margarine, softened
- 2 tablespoons superfine sugar
- 1½ tablespoons dark brown sugar
- ½ teaspoon ground cinnamon
- 2 tablespoons dairy-free butter/margarine, melted, for greasing the pan and coating the rolls

Frosting
- 3 tablespoons dairy-free cream cheese
- 1 teaspoon vanilla extract
- 2½ cups (300 g) confectioners' sugar, sifted
- ½ teaspoon ground cinnamon
- 2 teaspoons dairy-free milk

ROLLS

1. Place the milk and butter or margarine in a small saucepan and simmer over low heat until the butter or margarine has melted. Make sure it doesn't get too hot, as it could kill the yeast, which will make the dough less fluffy.

2. Pour the mixture into a bowl and sprinkle in the yeast and superfine sugar. Stir to combine. Cover with a tea towel and place in a warm area for the yeast to activate—this will take around 15 minutes. As the yeast activates, it will bubble and foam up.

3. Place the flour and ground cinnamon in a large bowl and pour over the activated yeast mixture. Mix together until a smooth dough forms—you can either do this with a wooden spoon or spatula, or in a stand mixer with a dough-hook attachment on low speed. The dough should form a ball and be slightly sticky.

4. Lightly grease a medium bowl with oil. Place the dough into the oiled bowl, cover with a tea towel, and place in a warm area for approximately 2 hours to rise. You want the dough to double in size.

5. Sprinkle flour over a clean worktop. Turn out the dough and knead lightly, then roll it out into a rectangle of approximately 14 by 8½ inches (35 by 22 cm), with the longer side nearer to you so it's easier to roll.

FILLING

1. Spread half the butter or margarine over the dough using a knife or spatula.

2. Combine the superfine sugar, brown sugar, and ground cinnamon in a small bowl. Sprinkle the cinnamon sugar over the buttered dough, covering it all, and then rub it in with your fingers. Press the sugar into the dough lightly with your hands. Spread the rest of the butter or margarine over the sugar.

THE ESSENTIAL BOOK OF VEGAN BAKES

3. Starting at the long side, tightly roll the dough into a log, pinching it as you go to keep it neat. Once in a log, cut it into 1- to 2-inch (2½ to 5 cm) rolls (see Tip). You may want to cut the ends off to keep it tidy.

4. Generously grease a 9-by-6-inch (23 by 15 cm) rectangular baking pan or dish with some of the melted butter or margarine and arrange the cinnamon rolls in it with the swirls facing up. Leave some space, about 1 inch (2½ cm), between them, as they will rise and fill the dish. Brush the rest of the melted butter or margarine over each roll.

5. Cover the rolls with a tea towel and place in a warm area. Leave them to rise for 20 minutes.

6. Preheat the oven to 400°F (200°C). Once the rolls have risen, place them in the middle of the oven and bake them for 20–25 minutes, or until golden (check them after 20 minutes).

7. Once baked, remove from the oven and set aside. You can enjoy them hot from the oven or warm with a cream cheese frosting.

FROSTING

1. In a medium mixing bowl, beat together the cream cheese and vanilla extract until light and creamy. You can use an electric hand mixer, food processor, or stand mixer with the balloon-whisk attachment (or you can use a wooden spoon, but it will take longer).

2. Add the confectioners' sugar and ground cinnamon and whip together until smooth. If the frosting is too thick, add the milk, a teaspoon at a time, to get it to the consistency of a thick paste.

3. Using a spoon or spatula, spread the frosting over the tops of the cinnamon rolls. If you do this when the cinnamon rolls are still warm, the frosting will soak into the rolls as opposed to sitting on top of them— delicious either way! Tear apart and enjoy.

These are best enjoyed on the day you make them; otherwise, you can store them in a sealed container in the fridge for a couple of days. Leave them at room temperature for an hour before serving.

Apricot Pinwheels

Everything tastes better when it's wrapped in puff pastry. These apricot pinwheels are a favorite in my family: crisp, flaky pastry bursting with fruity apricot flavor. You can customize this recipe by replacing the apricots with different fruits. Serve warm with a drizzle of cream or a scoop of ice cream. They can also be made gluten-free, if you use gluten-free, ready-to-roll pastry.

Makes 8 pinwheels

- 3 apricots, kernel removed
- 3 tablespoons superfine sugar, sifted
- 1 tablespoon cornstarch
- ¼ teaspoon ground cinnamon (optional)
- 1 sheet of ready-to-roll vegan puff pastry (gluten-free, if preferred)

Glaze
- Dairy-free milk
- Sprinkle of superfine sugar, to coat

HOLLY'S TIP

When they come out of the oven, you can brush them with some maple syrup to make them glossy and finger-licking good!

1. Chop the apricots into small pieces, then place them in a medium saucepan and sprinkle over the superfine sugar and cornstarch. Place the pan over medium heat. Once the apricots start to soften, use a potato masher or fork to mash them into a pulp. Simmer for around 10 minutes, stirring occasionally with a wooden spoon or spatula until the mixture has thickened. Once thickened, remove from the heat, stir in the ground cinnamon, and allow to cool (as it cools, the mixture will thicken more).

2. Preheat the oven to 400°F (200°C) and line a baking sheet with parchment paper (see page 17 for how to line a baking sheet). Unroll the puff pastry sheet onto a floured surface. Cut the pastry sheet into eight equal-sized squares.

3. Cut lines in each square from the corners almost to the middle. Spoon a tablespoon of the apricot mixture into the middle of each square. Fold each alternate corner over and press into the middle to create a pinwheel shape.

4. Brush some milk over the pastry pinwheels and sprinkle with some superfine sugar. Transfer to the lined baking sheet and bake in the center of the oven for 20–25 minutes, or until the pastry is golden brown. Allow to cool on a cooling rack.

Serve fresh on the day you make them.

Churros

The first things that pop into my mind when I think about churros are the cute little churro stands at fairs and theme parks, and the unmistakable smell of delicious deep-fried pastry wafting through the air. They should be crispy on the outside, soft on the inside, and topped with cinnamon sugar. You can eat these as they are or dunk them in warm chocolate ganache for extra indulgence.

Makes 35 (4-inch; 10 cm) churros

Churros
- 1⅔ cups (210 g) all-purpose flour, sifted
- 1 teaspoon baking powder
- 1 tablespoon sunflower oil
- 1 tablespoon superfine sugar
- 1⅔ cups (380 ml) water
- ¼ teaspoon salt
- 1 teaspoon vanilla extract
- Around 8½ cups (2 liters) sunflower oil, for deep-frying

Cinnamon sugar coating
- ½ cup (100 g) superfine sugar
- 1 tablespoon ground cinnamon

- Chocolate ganache (see page 201), to serve

HOLLY'S TIP

The dough is very tough to pipe, but persevere! And keep safety equipment on hand when using hot oil.

1. For the sugar coating, combine the superfine sugar and ground cinnamon in a bowl or shallow dish and set aside.

2. Line a baking sheet with parchment paper. In a large mixing bowl, mix the flour and baking powder until combined, then set aside.

3. Put the oil in a small saucepan along with the superfine sugar, water, salt, and vanilla extract. Bring to a boil over medium heat.

4. Once boiled, remove from the heat, then pour the liquid straight over the flour mixture and mix well with a wooden spoon or heatproof spatula until a dough forms. Leave the dough for about 10 minutes to cool slightly, as it will be very hot.

5. Place the dough in a piping bag fitted with a large star-tip nozzle and pipe 4-inch (10 cm) lines of dough onto the lined baking sheet (see Tip). Each time you pipe a line, snip the end of the dough from the piping bag with scissors.

6. Pour enough sunflower oil into a large saucepan or deep skillet to fill it half to three-quarters full. Heat to around 375°F (190°C). Remember to be extra cautious when using hot oil! If you don't have a candy or deep-fry thermometer, place the handle of a wooden spoon in the center of the hot oil. If the oil bubbles around the spoon, it is hot enough to use.

7. Lower the churros into the oil very carefully using a heatproof spatula 3–4 at a time (being careful not to overcrowd the pan). Fry on each side for about 2–3 minutes, or until golden brown. Transfer the churros to paper towels to soak up any excess oil, then roll them in the cinnamon sugar to coat. Watch to make sure the churros do not burn.

These are best served fresh and still warm with chocolate ganache. Once cool, they can be stored in an airtight container at room temperature for up to 2 days. You can reheat them in the oven for 5 minutes before serving.

Hot Cross Buns

This is my vegan take on the traditional spiced sweet bun. They're incredibly tasty (nobody is judging if you have more than one). I love mine toasted with a generous helping of dairy-free butter or margarine. *See photos on pages 86–87.*

Makes 12

Buns
- 3¾ cups (500 g) bread flour, plus extra for dusting
- 2½ teaspoons active dry yeast
- ¼ cup (50 g) superfine sugar
- 1¼ cup (175 g) mixed dried fruit
- 1 tablespoon allspice
- 1 teaspoon ground cinnamon
- ½ teaspoon nutmeg
- 2 tablespoons applesauce
- 2 tablespoons sunflower oil, plus extra for greasing
- ½ cup (125 ml) dairy-free milk
- ½ cup (125 ml) warm water

Cross and glaze
- 2 tablespoons all-purpose flour
- 1½ tablespoons water
- 3 tablespoons marmalade or apricot jam

HOLLY'S TIP

Swap the mixed dried fruit for your favorite dried fruit.

BUNS

1. In a large mixing bowl, mix together the flour, yeast, superfine sugar, mixed dried fruit, and spices. Then add the applesauce and mix with a wooden spoon until fully combined.

2. Add the oil, milk, and warm water. If you're using a stand mixer, attach a dough hook and mix until the mixture has formed into a sticky dough. If you're mixing by hand, use a wooden spoon or spatula.

3. Knead the dough until elastic and smooth—this will take around 10 minutes (or less if you're using a mixer with a dough hook).

4. Grease a large bowl with oil. Place the dough in the bowl and cover with a tea towel to stop the dough from forming a crust. Place the bowl in a warm area and leave to rise for around 1–2 hours, or until the dough has doubled in size.

5. Once the dough has risen, turn it out onto a lightly floured surface. Cut the dough into 12 equal-sized pieces. Carefully roll them into balls and place them in lines on a lightly oiled baking sheet or dish. You don't want to overwork the dough, as you will reduce the air it contains. Leave some room in between, as the buns will spread a little. Cover the baking sheet or dish with a tea towel and allow to proof for around an hour, or until the buns have risen.

6. Shortly before the buns have finished proofing, preheat the oven to 425°F (220°C) and make the cross mixture.

CROSS AND GLAZE

1. Place the flour and water in a bowl and mix until paste-like. Add a dash more water if needed. Transfer the mixture to a piping bag with a small round nozzle. (If you don't have a nozzle, you can snip the end off a disposable piping bag.)

2. When the buns have risen, pipe a line along each row, then repeat in the other direction to create a cross on each bun.

3. Place in the middle of the oven and bake for 15 minutes, or until the buns are golden.

4. Gently heat the marmalade or jam in a small saucepan and sift to remove any large chunks. Brush the warm preserve over the tops of the warm buns. Then they are ready to serve.

These are best served on the day you make them. Once cool, store in a sealed container at room temperature for up to 2 days (see Tip).

Scones

Scones are a hotbed of controversy—is it pronounced "scon" or "s-cone"? Do you top with jam or cream first? Or does it just not matter?! However you pronounce and eat them, I'm confident that opinion won't be divided by these delicious vegan scones.

Makes 8–10

Scones
- 3¼ cups (400 g) self-rising flour, plus extra for dusting
- ⅓ cup (60 g) superfine sugar
- 1 teaspoon baking powder
- ½ cup (120 g) dairy-free butter/margarine
- ¾ cup plus 1 tablespoon (200 ml) dairy-free milk
- 2 teaspoons vanilla extract

Glaze
- 1 teaspoon maple syrup
- 2 tablespoons dairy-free milk

- Dairy-free whipped cream and berry jam (see page 203), to serve

HOLLY'S TIP

You can add a handful of chocolate chips before baking for a chocolate treat!

SCONES

1. Preheat the oven to 425°F (220°C) and line a baking sheet with parchment paper (see page 17 for how to line a baking sheet). In a large mixing bowl, sift the flour, superfine sugar, and baking powder.

2. Using your fingers, rub in the butter or margarine until the mixture is crumbly.

3. Add the milk and vanilla extract. Mix with a wooden spoon until a dough forms. Bring the dough together to form a ball: it will be soft and sticky. Turn it out onto a lightly floured surface and lightly coat with flour.

4. Don't knead the dough: instead, use your hands to shape it to a thickness of about 2 inches (5 cm). It doesn't have to be perfect. Use a 2½-inch (6 cm) round cookie cutter to cut out the scones. Place them on the lined baking sheet, spacing them out, as they will spread a little.

GLAZE

1. Mix the maple syrup and milk in a bowl. Brush a little glaze over the top of each scone.

2. Place the scones in the center of the oven and bake for 15–20 minutes, or until golden brown (check them after 15 minutes). When baked, remove the scones from the oven.

Best served warm, straight from the oven, with a dollop of whipped cream and your favorite berry jam. These are best enjoyed on the day you make them.

Pink Strawberry Doughnuts

These doughnuts are going to be your new obsession. Oozing with strawberry jam and coated with pink sugar, they are perfect for Valentine's Day, but to be honest, there doesn't need to be a special occasion to enjoy them. I like to use gel food coloring in this recipe to make the doughnut hearts pink, but you can leave them plain if you prefer. *See photos on pages 92–93.*

Makes 15–18

Doughnuts
- 1⅓ cups plus 1 tablespoon (330 ml) dairy-free milk
- 4½ teaspoons active dry yeast
- ⅓ cup plus 1 tablespoon (75 g) superfine sugar
- 4¾ cups (600 g) self-rising flour, plus extra for dusting
- ¼ teaspoon salt
- ⅓ cup plus 1½ table-spoons (100 g) dairy-free butter/ margarine, melted
- 2 flax "eggs" (see egg replacements, page 15)
- Drop of pink gel food coloring (optional)
- Around 8½ cups (2 liters) sunflower oil, for deep-frying, plus extra for greasing the bowl

HOLLY'S TIP

If you don't have a heart-shaped cookie cutter, you can cut out the heart shapes using a knife.

DOUGHNUTS

1. Pour the milk into a small saucepan and place over low heat until it reaches a gentle simmer. Remove from the heat and pour the milk into a bowl. Sprinkle over the yeast and superfine sugar and stir to combine, then cover with a tea towel and leave in a warm place for around 10–15 minutes until frothy.

2. In a separate bowl, combine the flour and salt and stir. In another bowl, mix together the melted butter or margarine, flax "eggs," and a drop of pink gel food coloring, if using.

3. Combine the yeast mixture, the dry mixture, and the flax "egg" mixture together in a bowl and stir. Mix with an electric hand mixer or attach a dough hook to a stand mixer and begin to knead on low-medium speed until nice and smooth (knead by hand if you don't have a mixer). If it's too wet, add some more flour—you're looking for a soft, elastic dough.

4. Transfer the dough to a lightly oiled bowl. Cover with a tea towel and place in a warm area, then leave to proof for around 2–3 hours, or until doubled in size.

5. Line a baking sheet with parchment paper (see page 17 for how to line a baking sheet). Once the dough has doubled in size, turn it out onto a clean, floured surface and roll out to a thickness of around ½ inch (1¼ cm).

6. Using a medium heart-shaped cookie cutter, cut out dough hearts and place them on the lined baking sheet. Leave some room in between, as they will increase in size.

7. Return the baking sheet to the warm area and cover with a tea towel for around an hour until the hearts have doubled in size.

THE ESSENTIAL BOOK OF VEGAN BAKES

Coating and filling
- I cup (20 g) freeze-
  dried strawberries
- ½ cup (100 g) superfine
  sugar
- ¾ cup (250 g) strawberry
  jam (or make your own;
  see page 203)

8. Pour enough oil into a deep saucepan to fill it three-quarters full and bring to a boil over medium-high heat. Heat the oil to 360°F (182°C) This will take around 10 minutes. If you don't have a candy or deep-fry thermometer, place the handle of a wooden spoon in the center of the hot oil. If the oil bubbles around the spoon, it is hot enough to use. Remember to take extra care when using hot oil—and if you have long hair, you must tie it up!

9. Once the doughnuts have risen, carefully lower them into the hot oil one at a time using a heatproof spatula. You may get 3–4 in the pan at once, depending on the size of your pan. Fry for about 2–3 minutes on each side, or until puffed and golden brown. Wait for the oil to get back up to the correct temperature after each batch. Stay with the pan at all times to make sure the doughnuts do not burn.

10. Once golden, carefully remove them from the hot oil using a heatproof spatula and place on some paper towels to drain any excess oil. Repeat for all of the doughnuts, then set aside. Remember to take the hot oil off the heat when done.

COATING AND FILLING

1. Place the freeze-dried strawberries into a small blender and whizz up until they form a fine powder.

2. Now you're ready to coat the doughnuts! In a large bowl, mix together the superfine sugar and freeze-dried strawberry powder. Coat each heart doughnut in the pink sugar while they are still warm. Let the doughnuts cool before filling.

3. Put the strawberry jam into a piping bag with a small round-tip nozzle. If you don't have a piping bag, use a small spoon.

4. Poke a hole in the side or middle of each doughnut and fill it with as much or little jam filling as you like.

These are best served fresh on the day you make them.

Honeycomb Doughnuts

Doughnut worry, bee happy! These doughnuts are filled with a honeycomb cream and topped with crumbs of crunchy honeycomb. Have fun while making this recipe (but don't forget to be extra careful when using hot oil to deep-fry food). I'd suggest preparing the honeycomb before you start making the doughnuts, as it will need to cool fully before you use it. See page 194 for how to make vegan honeycomb—you will need a quarter of the honeycomb recipe. *See photo on page 96.*

Makes 18

Doughnuts
- 1⅓ cups plus 1 tablespoon (330 ml) dairy-free milk
- 4½ teaspoons active dry yeast
- ⅓ cup plus 1 tablespoon (75 g) superfine sugar
- 4¾ cups (600 g) self-rising flour, plus extra for dusting
- ¼ teaspoon salt
- ⅓ cup plus 1½ tablespoons (100 g) dairy-free butter/margarine, melted
- 2 flax "eggs" (see egg replacements, page 15)
- Around 8½ cups (2 liters) sunflower oil, for deep-frying, plus extra for greasing the bowl

Honeycomb cream filling and coating
- 1 cup (200 g) superfine sugar, for coating
- ⅓ cup (40 g) dairy-free whipping cream
- ¼ cup (50 g) dairy-free cream cheese
- 2½ cups (300 g) confectioners' sugar, sifted
- 2 ounces (60 g) honeycomb (see page 194; use ¼ of the recipe)

DOUGHNUTS

1. Pour the milk into a small saucepan and place over low heat until it reaches a gentle simmer. Remove from the heat and pour the milk into a bowl. Sprinkle in the yeast and superfine sugar and stir to combine, then cover with a tea towel and leave in a warm place for around 10–15 minutes until frothy.

2. In a separate bowl, combine the flour and salt and stir. In another bowl, mix together the melted butter or margarine and flax "eggs."

3. Combine the yeast mixture, the dry mixture, and the flax "egg" mixture together in a bowl and stir. Mix with an electric hand mixer or attach a dough hook to a stand mixer and begin to knead on low-medium speed until nice and smooth (knead by hand if you don't have a mixer). If it's too wet, add some more flour—you're looking for a soft, elastic dough.

4. Transfer the dough to a lightly oiled bowl. Cover with a tea towel and place in a warm area, then leave to proof for around 2–3 hours, or until doubled in size.

5. Line a baking sheet with parchment paper (see page 17 for how to line a baking sheet). Once the dough has doubled in size, turn it out onto a clean, floured surface and roll out to a thickness of around ½ inch (1¼ cm).

6. Using a 2-inch (5 cm) round cookie cutter, cut out circles of the dough and place on the lined baking sheet. Cover with a tea towel and return to the warm area for around an hour, or until they have doubled in size.

7. Pour enough oil into a deep saucepan to fill it three-quarters full and bring to a boil over medium-high heat. Heat the oil to 360°F (182°C). This will take around 10 minutes. If you don't have a candy or deep-fry

thermometer, place the handle of a wooden spoon in the center of the hot oil. If the oil bubbles around the spoon, it is hot enough to use. Remember to take extra care when using hot oil—and if you have long hair, you must tie it up!

8. Once the doughnuts have risen, carefully lower them into the hot oil one at a time using a heatproof spatula. You may get 3–4 in the pan at once, depending on the size of your pan. Fry for about 2–3 minutes on each side, or until puffed and golden brown. Wait for the oil to get back up to the correct temperature after each batch. Stay with the pan at all times to make sure the doughnuts do not burn.

9. Once golden, carefully remove them from the hot oil using a heatproof spatula and place on some paper towels to drain any excess oil. Repeat for all of the doughnuts. Remember to take the hot oil off the heat when done.

HONEYCOMB CREAM FILLING AND COATING

1. Spread the superfine sugar on a baking sheet and coat the doughnuts in the sugar while they are still warm. Set aside and leave them to cool fully before filling.

2. Cream the whipping cream and cream cheese together until creamy— you can use an electric hand mixer, a stand mixer with a balloon-whisk attachment, or a wooden spoon (but the spoon will take you longer).

3. Add the confectioners' sugar and whip together until smooth. You want this filling to be quite thick. If it's too runny, add more confectioners' sugar.

4. Finely crumble most of the honeycomb into the cream filling and whip until combined (you don't want huge chunks of honeycomb, as this would make it hard to pipe into the doughnuts).

5. Transfer the cream filling to a piping bag fitted with a large pastry or open star-tip nozzle. Poke a hole in the side or middle of each doughnut and fill with as much or as little cream filling as you like. Top each doughnut with a piece of honeycomb just before serving.

Serve fresh and enjoy! These are best eaten on the day you make them.

Cookies-and-Cream Macarons

Macarons are dainty, cream-filled cookie sandwiches that have those infamous ruffles around the edges called "feet." Transport your imagination to the cobbled streets of Paris with one bite. Here you get double the deliciousness with these cookies-and-cream macarons! *See photo on page 97.*

Makes around 20 (1¾-inch; 4½ cm) sandwiched macarons

Macaron shells
- 1 cup (110 g) ground almonds/almond flour, sifted
- ¾ cup plus 2½ tablespoons (110 g) confectioners' sugar, sifted
- ⅓ cup (75 g) aquafaba
- ¼ teaspoon cream of tartar
- ⅓ cup (65 g) superfine sugar
- ½ vegan chocolate cream cookie, finely crumbled (I use Oreos)

Filling
- 3 tablespoons (40 g) dairy-free butter/margarine
- 1 tablespoon aquafaba
- 5 vegan chocolate cream cookies (I use Oreos), finely crumbled
- 1⅓ cups plus 1 tablespoon (175 g) confectioners' sugar, sifted

MACARON SHELLS

1. Line two baking sheets with parchment paper (see page 17 for how to line a baking sheet, and see the Tip on templates on page 99). Combine the almond flour/ground almonds and confectioners' sugar together in a bowl and set aside.

2. Place the aquafaba and the cream of tartar into a mixing bowl and whizz on high speed for around 5 minutes until the mixture is white and holds soft peaks. I use a stand mixer with a balloon-whisk attachment, but you can also use an electric hand mixer.

3. Gradually add in the superfine sugar a little at a time while it is mixing on high speed. After around 5 minutes, it will turn thick, glossy, and hold stiff peaks. Mix in the sifted ground almonds and confectioners' sugar. Using a rubber spatula, slowly fold the dry ingredients into the meringue mixture until just incorporated. You want to be gentle during this stage. Fold it in a J shape (scrape around the sides of the bowl, then down the middle, and repeat). Check to see if it's ready by scooping up some of the mixture using a spatula and drizzling it back into the bowl. It shouldn't form a continuous ribbon but it should ribbon a little bit and then separate in chunks. If you get to the ribbon stage, you've gone too far.

4. Transfer the mixture to a piping bag fitted with a large round-tip nozzle, or snip the end off a disposable piping bag, and pipe 1¾-inch (4½ cm) circles onto the parchment paper (see Tip). Hold the piping bag vertically, applying even pressure, and squeeze until you have a circle of the correct size, then swirl the tip to one side and repeat. Make sure to space them out a little.

5. With your finger, gently push down any macaron batter that is sticking up, then tap the baking sheets firmly on the worktop 2 or 3 times to release any air bubbles. Sprinkle the crumbled cookie over the macarons.

THE ESSENTIAL BOOK OF VEGAN BAKES

HOLLY'S TIP

To get all the macarons the same size, print a template off the internet and lay it under the parchment paper, but remove before baking.

HOLLY'S TIP

It's key to get the exact measurements when creating macarons— I'd recommend weighing in grams rather than measuring in cups.

6. Allow the macarons to stand at room temperature for 1–1½ hours, until you can touch the top of them and none of the mixture comes off on your finger. Drying time may vary depending on the humidity of the atmosphere.

7. Preheat the oven to 275°F (140°C) just before they are ready. Bake the macarons, one sheet at a time, in the center of the preheated oven for around 20 minutes. The baking time may vary depending on your oven and the consistency of the mixture. Rotate the baking sheet every 5 minutes to ensure an even bake. You will know they are done when they peel away from the parchment paper and have a smooth base. Be careful, as they are fragile at this stage.

8. Once baked, remove from the oven and leave them on the baking sheet to cool fully before removing and filling.

FILLING

1. Using an electric hand mixer, a hand mixer, or a stand mixer with a balloon-whisk attachment, cream the butter or margarine on high speed until light and fluffy. This will take a few minutes. Add the aquafaba and cookie crumbs. Sift in the confectioners' sugar. Mix until it is creamy and pipeable.

2. Transfer the buttercream to a piping bag fitted with a star-tip nozzle. Add a swirl of buttercream to one macaron shell and sandwich it by placing another shell on top. Repeat with the remaining shells and filling.

Store the macarons in the fridge in a sealed container for up to 7 days or in the freezer for a month. When storing, you don't want any moisture to get into the macarons, as it can ruin them.

Mince Pies

I love relaxing on the sofa at Christmas with a warm mince pie in hand, watching a Harry Potter movie marathon. Molly Weasley sends Harry a dozen home-baked mince pies for Christmas one year—if they tasted half as good as these, then I'm sure Harry would have devoured them all in one sitting!

Makes 6–8

Pastry
- 1⅔ cups (200 g) all-purpose flour
- ½ cup plus 1 tablespoon (80 g) coconut oil, melted, plus extra for greasing
- 4 tablespoons maple syrup

Filling
- Jar of vegan-friendly mincemeat

- Confectioners' sugar, for dusting

HOLLY'S TIP

As the pans are greased, the pies should slide out of the pan easily, but if not, run a knife around the edge of the wells, then lift them out.

PASTRY

1. Preheat the oven to 400°F (200°C). In a mixing bowl, combine the flour, melted coconut oil, and maple syrup. Mix and bring together with your hands or a wooden spoon until a dough forms. If the dough is too sticky, add more flour—you want it to resemble pastry.

2. Roll about 3 tablespoons of the dough between two sheets of parchment paper until 1/16-inch (2 mm) thick. Using mini cookie cutters or a sharp knife, cut out festive shapes for the tops of the mince pies and set aside.

3. Lightly grease two cupcake pans with coconut oil. Press 2 tablespoons of dough into each cupcake well, molding the dough up the sides to create a cup. Prick the bases with a fork and place in the oven to bake for 5 minutes.

4. Remove the pans from the oven. Fill each pastry with 2 tablespoons of mincemeat and top with a pastry shape. Return to the oven for a further 12–14 minutes, or until golden. Place the pans on a cooling rack and allow the pies to cool in the pan before lifting them out.

Serve with a dusting of confectioners' sugar. Store in a sealed container. These are best eaten within a few days of making.

COOKIES AND BARS

White Chocolate and Cashew Cookies

With crisp edges and a gooey, chewy center, these cookies are devilishly moreish. All you need to serve them with is an ice-cold glass of your favorite dairy-free milk for dunking.

Makes 12 cookies

- ⅓ cup plus 2½ table-spoons (110 g) dairy-free butter/margarine, softened
- ½ cup (100 g) superfine sugar
- ¼ cup (50 g) light brown sugar
- 1 teaspoon vanilla extract
- 1⅓ cups plus 2 table-spoons (180 g) all-purpose flour
- 1 teaspoon baking soda
- 1 tablespoon dairy-free milk
- ¼ cup plus 1 tablespoon (50 g) dairy-free white chocolate, plus 2½ tablespoons for topping, roughly chopped
- ⅓ cup plus 1 tablespoon (50 g) cashews, plus 1 tablespoon for topping, roughly chopped

1. Preheat the oven to 400°F (200°C) and line two baking sheets with parchment paper (see page 17 for how to line a baking sheet). Add the softened butter or margarine, superfine sugar, light brown sugar, and vanilla extract to a mixing bowl and cream together—you can use a wooden spoon or a stand mixer with a paddle attachment.

2. Sift the flour and baking soda into the butter or margarine mixture and mix together until crumbly. Add the milk and mix to create a thick cookie dough.

3. Add the chopped white chocolate and the chopped cashews to the dough and mix. Your cookie dough will be very thick but sticky enough to easily roll into balls.

4. Roll into small balls of (about 1 heaped tablespoon; 40 g each) and space out evenly on the lined baking sheets. Press down only slightly to flatten the tops (not too much—you still want them to be ball-like). The cookies will spread out a lot, so give them room. Before baking, press the remaining chopped nuts and white chocolate into the tops of the cookies.

5. Bake for 10 minutes in the center of the oven. When they come out of the oven, the edges of the cookies will be firm, but they will still be soft in the middle. This is fine, as they will firm up as they cool down and set. Leave on the baking sheet to cool down.

These are best enjoyed on the day you make them. Store in a sealed container at room temperature and eat within a few days.

HOLLY'S TIP

To make the cookies equal-sized, place a cookie cutter of a similar size around each cookie and nudge to shape them as they come out of the oven.

Pecan Cookies

These pecan cookies are loaded with buttery pecan flavor and a surprise chocolate center. Serve them warm for the best results, as the chocolate center will be soft and gooey. Customize this recipe by removing the chocolate or replacing the pecans with any nut of your choice.

Makes 10–11 cookies

- 2 cups (250 g) all-purpose flour
- 1 teaspoon baking powder
- ¼ cup (50 g) superfine sugar
- ⅓ cup plus 2 tablespoons (100 g) coconut oil, melted
- 1 teaspoon vanilla extract
- 1 flax "egg" (see egg replacements, page 15)
- 2 tablespoons maple syrup
- ⅔ cup (80 g) pecans, finely chopped, plus 10–11 whole pecans, to decorate
- ¼ cup plus 1 tablespoon (50 g) dairy-free dark chocolate chunks

1. Preheat the oven to 400°F (200°C) and line a baking sheet with parchment paper (see page 17 for how to line a baking sheet).

2. In a medium bowl, combine the flour, baking powder, and superfine sugar. In a separate bowl, combine the melted coconut oil, vanilla extract, flax "egg," and maple syrup.

3. Add the dry mixture to the wet and combine fully with a wooden spoon, then fold in the chopped pecans. You may want to use your hands to bring the dough together.

4. Using the palms of your hands, roll the cookie dough into golf ball–sized balls (about 2 level tablespoons; 50 g). Flatten the middle of each doughball slightly to create a doughnut shape and add a dark chocolate chunk (about 1 teaspoon) into the middle. Then wrap the cookie dough around the chocolate fully, so it's enclosed, and roll it back into a ball.

5. Place the cookie balls 2 inches (5 cm) apart on the lined baking sheet. Press down slightly to flatten and lightly press a pecan onto the top of each cookie. The cookies will spread out slightly but not a lot.

6. Place in the center of the oven and bake for 12–15 minutes, or until golden. Once baked, carefully place the cookies onto a cooling rack and allow to cool fully (they will firm up as they cool).

Store in a sealed container at room temperature. Best eaten within a few days of making.

THE ESSENTIAL BOOK OF VEGAN BAKES

Funfetti Cookies

The word *funfetti* originated in the UK in the 1980s and literally means "fun" and "confetti"—funfetti! These cookies are the kind of treats that put a smile on everyone's face, no matter what age. It's impossible to frown when you've got one of my funfetti cookies in your hand. *See photo on page 110.*

Makes 10 cookies

- ⅔ cup (120 g) superfine sugar
- ⅓ cup (80 g) dairy-free butter/margarine
- 1 tablespoon dairy-free milk
- 1 teaspoon vanilla extract
- 1¼ cups (160 g) all-purpose flour
- ½ teaspoon baking powder
- 3 tablespoons vegan rainbow sprinkles, plus extra for topping (optional)

HOLLY'S TIP

Source some bold, brightly colored sprinkles so they can be seen in your bakes (natural sprinkles lose their color during baking).

1. Preheat the oven to 400°F (200°C). Line a baking sheet with parchment paper (see page 17 for how to line a baking sheet). In a large bowl, cream the superfine sugar, butter or margarine, milk, and vanilla extract together.

2. Add the flour and baking powder and stir with a wooden spoon to combine into a cookie dough. Add a splash more milk if the mixture is too thick, or add more flour if it's too wet—the dough should be thick enough to roll. Gently fold in the sprinkles. Don't overmix or you'll lose the vibrant sprinkle colors. Bring the dough together using your hands.

3. Roll into small balls (about 1 heaped tablespoon; 40 g each) and space evenly apart on the baking sheet—the cookies will spread during baking, so give them plenty of room. Press each one down slightly to flatten. Lightly press some more sprinkles, if using, over the top of the cookies. Place in the center of the oven and bake for 15–18 minutes, or until lightly golden. Remove from the oven and allow the cookies to cool completely on the baking sheet (they will firm up as they cool).

These are best enjoyed on the day you make them. Store in a sealed container at room temperature and eat within a few days.

THE ESSENTIAL BOOK OF VEGAN BAKES

Double Chocolate Cookies

How do you make chocolate even better? You double it! There is something so dreamy about finding a bakery that serves fresh batches of the most amazing-smelling chocolate chip cookies. I simply had to perfect my own bakery-style Double Chocolate Cookies—slightly crunchy on the outside, and soft and gooey on the inside. *See photo on page 111.*

Makes 15 cookies

- ⅓ cup plus 2½ table-spoons (110 g) dairy-free butter/margarine
- ¾ cup (150 g) superfine sugar
- ¼ cup (50 g) light brown sugar
- 1 teaspoon vanilla extract
- 1⅓ cups (170 g) all-purpose flour
- ¼ cup (30 g) cocoa powder
- 1 teaspoon baking soda
- 1 tablespoon dairy-free milk
- 1 cup plus 3 tablespoons (200 g) dairy-free dark chocolate chips or small chunks, plus extra for topping (optional)

HOLLY'S TIP
To make the cookies equal-sized, place a cookie cutter of a similar size around each cookie and nudge them into shape as they come out of the oven.

1. Preheat the oven to 400°F (200°C) and line two baking sheets with parchment paper (see page 17 for how to line a sheet). Cream together the butter or margarine, superfine sugar, and light brown sugar in a mixing bowl—you can use a wooden spoon and a mixing bowl, a food processor, or a stand mixer with a paddle attachment. Mix (on low if using a processor or stand mixer) until creamy. Add the vanilla extract and mix in.

2. Sift the flour, cocoa powder, and baking soda into a separate bowl. Add the dry ingredients to the butter or margarine mixture and mix together until crumbly.

3. Add in the milk and mix into a thick cookie dough. Add the chocolate chips or chunks and mix them in. The cookie dough will be very thick, and you may need to use your hands to bring it together.

4. Using your hands, roll into small balls (about 1 heaped tablespoon; 45 g) each and space them evenly apart on the lined baking sheets. Press each cookie down slightly with the palm of your hand to flatten. These cookies will spread out a lot, so give them room!

5. Bake for 10 minutes. The edges of the cookies will be firm, but they will still be very soft in the middle. Press a few more dark chocolate chips or chunks onto the tops of the cookies as they come out of the oven, if you like. Leave the cookies on the baking sheets to cool (they will firm up as they cool). If the chocolate is too gooey, pop them into the fridge to set.

These are best enjoyed on the day you make them. Store in a sealed container at room temperature and eat within a few days.

Golden Syrup Flapjacks

As a child, I used to love baking chewy, oaty flapjacks with my mom, and they're still one of my favorite baked goods—simple to make yet such a tasty treat. Customize these by adding extra ingredients, such as chocolate chips, dried fruit, coconut flakes, or even cinnamon for a bit of festive warmth.

Makes around 14 flapjacks

- 3⅓ cups (300 g) gluten-free whole or rolled oats
- ⅓ cup plus 1 tablespoon (80 g) light brown sugar
- 4 tablespoons golden syrup
- 1 teaspoon vanilla extract
- ½ cup plus 1 tablespoon (130 g) dairy-free butter/margarine

1. Preheat the oven to 400°F (200°C) and line an 8-inch (20 cm) square baking pan with parchment paper (see page 17 for how to line a pan).

2. Place the oats, light brown sugar, golden syrup, vanilla extract, and butter or margarine in a food processor and pulse until combined—don't overmix, as you want the oats to retain some texture.

3. Spoon the mixture into the lined pan, then spread it out and compact it. Bake for 15–20 minutes, or until golden. Once baked, remove from the oven and leave to cool in the pan before slicing.

Store in an airtight container in the fridge. Leave at room temperature for 15 minutes before serving. Best eaten within a week of making.

Peanut Butter Swirl Flapjacks

I love this combination of oats, chocolate, and peanut butter. These flapjacks are picture-perfect, unbelievably delicious, and so easy to whip up.

Makes 14 flapjacks

Base
- 4½ cups (400 g) whole or rolled gluten-free oats
- ⅓ cup plus 2 tablespoons (90 g) light brown sugar
- 3 tablespoons smooth peanut butter
- 3 tablespoons golden syrup
- ¾ cup (180 g) dairy-free butter/margarine

Chocolate topping and peanut butter swirl
- 1 cup plus 3 tablespoons (200 g) dairy-free chocolate
- ½ teaspoon coconut oil
- 2 tablespoons smooth peanut butter

BASE

1. Preheat the oven to 400°F (200°C) and line an 8-inch (20 cm) square baking pan with parchment paper (see page 17 for how to line a pan). Allow the paper to hang on either side of the pan; this makes it easier to remove the flapjack after baking. Place the oats, light brown sugar, peanut butter, golden syrup, and butter or margarine in a food processor and pulse until combined. Be careful not to overmix—you want the oats to retain some texture.

2. Spoon the mixture into the lined pan and spread it out until flat, making sure the mixture is compact and reaches the corners. Bake for 15–20 minutes, or until golden. Once baked, remove from the oven and leave to cool in the pan before adding the topping.

CHOCOLATE TOPPING AND PEANUT BUTTER SWIRL

1. Melt the chocolate and coconut oil using a bain-marie (see page 17) or in the microwave. Pour this mixture over the flapjack, using a spoon or spatula to spread it evenly and into each corner.

2. While the chocolate is still soft, melt the peanut butter in the same way and, using a spoon, dollop small drops of it onto the chocolate in random places. Using a toothpick or skewer, swirl the melted peanut butter and chocolate together—don't overswirl or you will lose the marble effect. Place the flapjack in the fridge for an hour to set.

3. When the chocolate has set, lift the flapjack out of the pan and place on a chopping board. Then, using a sharp knife, slice it into squares, cutting them as big or small as you'd like.

Store in the fridge in a sealed container and leave at room temperature for 15 minutes before serving. Best eaten within a week of making.

Shortbread

My sweet and crisp shortbread recipe uses only three simple ingredients that you might have in your cupboard already. They taste best when eaten fresh and warm out of the oven. If you have children, they'll love decorating these.

Makes 18 cookies

- 2½ cups plus 1 tablespoon (320 g) all-purpose flour, plus extra for dusting
- ½ cup (100 g) superfine sugar, plus extra for sprinkling after baking
- 1 cup plus 1 tablespoon (240 g) dairy-free butter/ margarine

1. Preheat the oven to 400°F (200°C) and line a baking sheet with parchment paper (see page 17 for how to line a baking sheet). Place the flour and superfine sugar in a bowl and combine with a wooden spoon.

2. Add the butter or margarine, and rub together with your fingers until a dough forms. Place the dough in a bowl, then cover and put it in the fridge for 20 minutes (this makes it easier to roll and cut out). The dough should be slightly sticky, but it should not stick to your hands.

3. Roll out the dough on a floured surface or between two sheets of parchment paper to a thickness of about ½ inch (1¼ cm). Cut the cookies into 2½-inch (6 cm) squares and place them on the lined baking sheet (the shortbread will not spread out). If you don't have a square cookie cutter, you can cut them by hand or use a round cookie cutter. Place in the oven and bake for 20 minutes, or until golden brown. Sprinkle with some superfine sugar while still warm.

Indulge in them right away or allow to cool fully before storing them in a sealed container at room temperature. Best eaten within a couple of weeks.

Lemon Swirl Cookies

My take on the classic Viennese whirl, these incredibly tasty swirl cookies are complemented by a creamy lemon filling. If you prefer, you can leave out the filling and enjoy the cookies on their own. *See photo on page 120.*

Makes 20 cookies or 10 sandwiched cookies

Cookies
- ¾ cup plus 2 tablespoons (200 g) dairy-free block butter (not margarine), room temperature
- ⅔ cup (80 g) confectioners' sugar, sifted
- 3 tablespoons lemon juice
- 1 tablespoon lemon zest
- ¼ teaspoon baking powder
- 2¼ cups (280 g) all-purpose flour, sifted
- Superfine sugar, for sprinkling (optional)

Filling
- ¼ cup (50 g) dairy-free cream cheese
- 1½ tablespoons dairy-free block butter (not margarine)
- 1 tablespoon lemon juice
- 2 cups plus 1 tablespoon (250 g) confectioners' sugar, sifted

- A sprinkling of confectioners' sugar and lemon zest, to dust (optional)

COOKIES

1. Preheat the oven to 400°F (200°C) and line two baking sheets with parchment paper (see page 17 for how to line a baking sheet). In a large bowl, cream the butter and confectioners' sugar together until light in color—you can either use a stand mixer with a paddle attachment, an electric hand mixer, or a wooden spoon, but the spoon will take you longer.

2. Add the lemon juice and zest. Mix together until fully combined. Add the baking powder to the flour. Then, add this to the butter and sugar mixture in two stages, mixing on high if using a stand mixer, until a sticky dough forms and is of pipable consistency. Add a little more lemon juice, if needed, to get it to the right consistency.

3. Transfer the dough to a piping bag fitted with a large star-tip nozzle. As it's not a runny mixture, you will have to apply some pressure when piping. Pipe 2½-inch (6 cm) swirls onto the lined sheets, leaving a little space in between each cookie. Repeat until you've used up all the mixture—you should end up with around 20 cookies in total.

4. Sprinkle some superfine sugar and lemon zest over each cookie, if you like. Place the baking sheets in the middle of the oven and bake for 12 minutes, or until the cookies are lightly golden.

5. Remove from the oven and leave the cookies to cool slightly on the baking sheets, then use a spatula to transfer them to a wire rack to cool fully.

FILLING

1. In a medium bowl, cream together the cream cheese and butter until light in color—you can use a stand mixer with a balloon-whisk attachment, an electric hand mixer, a food processor, or a wooden spoon.

2. Add the lemon juice and confectioners' sugar, then whisk together until creamy. This will take around 5 minutes on high speed if you're using an electric whisk or stand mixer—if you're using a wooden spoon, it may take a little longer. If the frosting is too thick, add a splash more lemon juice; if it's too runny, add more confectioners' sugar. You're after a thick and creamy consistency.

3. Transfer the filling to a piping bag fitted with a star-tip nozzle. Turn half the cookies upside down so their flat side is facing upward. Pipe a swirl of the filling over them and sandwich the other cookies on top with the flat sides in the middle. Repeat until all of the cookies are sandwiched.

Store them in a sealed container in the fridge. Serve with a dusting of confectioners' sugar and a sprinkling of lemon zest, if using. These are best eaten within a few days.

Lemon Cookies with Strawberry Jam Filling

I have fond memories of being a child and twisting open Jammie Dodgers (popular British cookies) to lick the delicious jam inside! This is my take on a Jammie Dodger, which is traditionally made with shortbread and a raspberry jam filling. My recipe features buttery lemon-flavored cookies and a center of sweet and fruity strawberry jam. Get creative with different cookie cutters for any occasion! *See photo on page 121.*

Makes 10 sandwich cookies

Cookies
- 2 cups (250 g) all-purpose flour, plus extra for dusting
- ¼ cup (50 g) superfine sugar
- 1 tablespoon lemon zest, finely grated
- 1 teaspoon vanilla extract
- ⅔ cup (150 g) dairy-free butter/margarine
- 1 tablespoon dairy-free milk

Filling
- Strawberry jam (you can make your own using the recipe on page 203)

- Confectioner's sugar, for dusting

HOLLY'S TIP

Experiment with any cutters you may have. I chose stars because they remind me of Christmas.

COOKIES

1. Preheat the oven to 400°F (200°C) and line two baking sheets with parchment paper (see page 17 for how to line a baking sheet). In a medium bowl, mix together the flour, superfine sugar, and lemon zest with a wooden spoon to combine.

2. Add the vanilla extract, butter or margarine, and milk. Bring the ingredients together and knead lightly until a smooth dough forms—you can either use your hands or a wooden spoon.

3. Form the dough into a ball and wrap it in parchment paper. Place in the freezer for 10 minutes to firm up slightly (this makes it easier to roll out and cut out the cookie shapes).

4. Turn the dough out onto a lightly floured surface or place it in between two sheets of parchment paper. Using a rolling pin, roll it out to a thickness of around ⅛ inch (3 mm). Using a 3-inch (7 cm) round or fluted cookie cutter, cut out 20 cookies and, using a flat spatula or palette knife, place them on the lined baking sheets (these cookies won't spread during baking).

5. Using a smaller cookie cutter, cut out the centers of half of the cookies. You can bake the little cut-out shapes and enjoy them as a snack or combine them with any remnants of dough and reroll to make a few extra sandwich cookies.

THE ESSENTIAL BOOK OF VEGAN BAKES

6. Place the baking sheets in the middle of the oven and bake for 8–10 minutes, or until the cookies are golden. If your oven can only fit one sheet on the middle rack, bake one sheet at a time so all of the cookies bake evenly. When the cookies have turned golden, remove them from the oven and place the sheets on a cooling rack. Allow to cool fully before filling.

FILLING

1. Spoon 1 teaspoon of strawberry jam into the middle of the whole cookie, then sandwich each one with a cookie with the center cut out (when you do this, the hole will fill up with jam). Repeat for all of the cookies. Dust with confectioners' sugar, if using.

These are best stored in a sealed container at room temperature and eaten within a few days of making.

Coconut Macaroons

You'll go coco-nuts for my coconut macaroons! Sweet and sticky domes of coconut, crisp and golden on the outside, soft and chewy on the inside—they're delicious plain but even more irresistible drizzled with and dipped in chocolate. I've made this recipe gluten-free, but you can use regular all-purpose flour if you'd prefer.

Makes 15 macaroons

- 2¾ cups plus 1 tablespoon (230 g) shredded coconut
- ⅔ cup (140 g) thick coconut cream (see Tip)
- 1 tablespoon maple syrup
- 1 tablespoon vanilla extract
- 1 cup (200 g) superfine sugar
- 1 cup (125 g) gluten-free all-purpose flour
- ¾ cup plus 1 tablespoon (130 g) dairy-free dark chocolate

HOLLY'S TIP

You can extract coconut cream from a can of coconut milk. See page 14 for a description of how to do this.

1. Preheat the oven to 375°F (190°C) and line a large baking sheet with parchment paper (see page 17 for how to line a baking sheet). In a bowl, mix together the shredded coconut, coconut cream, maple syrup, vanilla extract, superfine sugar, and flour with a wooden spoon (the mixture should be sticky).

2. Using a 2-inch (5 cm) ice cream scoop or a spoon, form the mixture into mounds on the lined baking sheet, making sure you space them about 1 inch (2½ cm) apart. Bake for 15–18 minutes, or until golden brown on top.

3. Remove the baking sheet from the oven and place on a cooling rack. Allow the macaroons to cool fully on the sheet before decorating. They will be fragile when they're hot, so allow them to set and cool fully before moving them.

4. Melt the dairy-free chocolate until smooth using a bain-marie (see page 17) or the microwave. Dip the bases of the macaroons in the melted chocolate, letting any excess drip back into the bowl, then return the macaroons to the lined baking sheets, base side down.

5. Using a spoon, zigzag any excess chocolate over the tops of the macaroons. Place them in the fridge for about 10 minutes to allow the chocolate to set.

Store in a sealed container in the fridge. These are best enjoyed within a few days of making.

Mint Chocolate Thins

My mint chocolate thins feature a crisp chocolate and peppermint cookie encased in smooth minty chocolate that will have you coming back again and again. Enjoy at any time of year, but I particularly love to make these for the festive season. It's preferable to temper the chocolate for the coating (see how on page 207), but if you'd rather not, simply follow the steps below.

Makes 20 cookies

Cookies
- 1⅔ cups (200 g) all-purpose flour
- ¼ cup (30 g) cocoa powder
- ⅓ cup plus 2 tablespoons (100 g) coconut oil, melted
- 3 tablespoons maple syrup
- ½ teaspoon peppermint extract

Chocolate coating
- 1⅓ cups plus 2½ table-spoons (250 g) dairy-free chocolate chips or broken-up chunks
- 1 teaspoon peppermint extract
- 1 teaspoon coconut oil

HOLLY'S TIP

Put some flour on the worktop and coat the bottom of the cutter before each use. This helps prevent the cutter from sticking to the dough.

COOKIES

1. Preheat the oven to 400°F (200°C) and line a large baking sheet with parchment paper (see page 17 for how to line a sheet).

2. In a large mixing bowl, mix together the flour, cocoa powder, melted coconut oil, maple syrup, and peppermint extract. Combine with a spoon to form a smooth dough.

3. Between two sheets of parchment paper, roll the dough to a thickness of ¼ inch (½ cm). Using a 2½-inch (6 cm) round cookie cutter, cut out circles and place them on the lined baking sheet. Reroll any excess dough you have and repeat until you've used it all up. You should have 20 cookies.

4. Bake for around 10 minutes, then remove from the oven and leave to cool completely on the baking sheet before coating.

CHOCOLATE COATING

1. Temper the chocolate according to the instructions on page 207, or simply use a bain-marie (see page 17) to melt it. Once melted, take it off the heat and stir in the peppermint extract and coconut oil.

2. Balance a cookie on the tines of a fork and lower it into the chocolate, turning it to make sure it's completely coated. Lift it out and place it back on the baking sheet. Tap the fork on the side of the bowl to allow any excess chocolate to drip back into the bowl. Repeat for all of the cookies.

3. Place the thins in the fridge to set. This will take around 20 minutes. Cut away any excess chocolate from around the cookies before serving.

If the chocolate has been tempered, the thins can be left at room temperature; otherwise, keep them in a sealed container in the fridge. They're best enjoyed within a week of making.

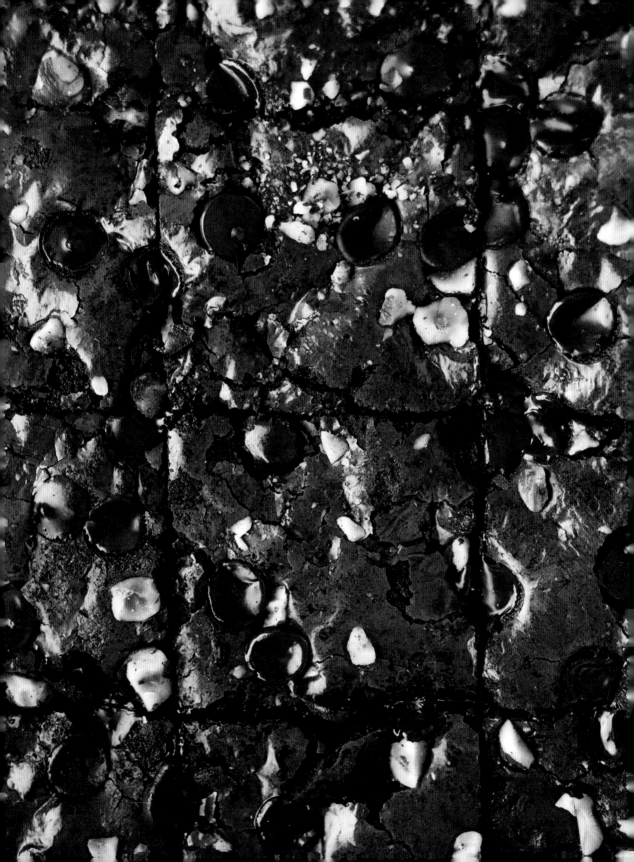

Chocolate and Hazelnut Brownies

Nutty, chocolaty, crisp on the outside, gooey on the inside, and perfectly indulgent. This is everything you want in a brownie. Simply leave out the hazelnuts for a nut-free version.

Makes 12 brownies

- 2 tablespoons milled flaxseed/linseed
- 2 tablespoons water
- ¼ cup (40 g) dairy-free dark chocolate
- ½ cup (115 g) dairy-free butter/margarine
- ¾ cup plus 1 tablespoon (160 g) superfine sugar
- ⅓ cup (50 g) cocoa powder
- ½ teaspoon vanilla extract
- ¾ teaspoon baking powder
- ¾ cup plus 3 tablespoons (115 g) all-purpose flour
- ¼ cup plus 1 tablespoon (50 g) dairy-free dark chocolate chips
- 2 tablespoons (20 g) hazelnuts, roughly chopped

HOLLY'S TIP

Brownies tend to taste fudgier on the second day after making.

1. Preheat the oven to 375°F (190°C) and line a 9-inch (22 cm) square baking pan with parchment paper (see page 17 for how to line a pan). Allow the paper to hang on either side of the pan so it's easier to remove the brownies once they're baked.

2. Mix the flaxseed with the water and set aside for 10 minutes to thicken. In a small saucepan, melt the chocolate and butter or margarine over low heat. Stir continuously until it's all melted together.

3. Add the flaxseed mixture, butter or margarine and chocolate mixture, the superfine sugar, cocoa powder, vanilla extract, and baking powder in a medium mixing bowl and mix with a wooden spoon or spatula for 1–2 minutes until fully incorporated and you have a thick chocolaty paste.

4. Sift in the flour and fold in with a spatula or wooden spoon until fully incorporated and a thick brownie mixture has formed.

5. Fold in three-quarters of the chocolate chips and three-quarters of the hazelnuts. Press the mixture into the pan using your fingers or a spoon. It needs to be flat and even. As the mixture is sticky, dip your fingertips in cocoa powder before pressing down to prevent the dough from sticking to your fingers. Scatter and press in the rest of the chocolate chips and chopped hazelnuts.

6. Place the pan in the middle of the oven and bake for 15 minutes. You don't want to overbake them or they lose their soft, fudgy texture. Remove from the oven and leave to cool fully in the pan before cutting into bars.

Store in a sealed container in the fridge. They will firm up in the fridge, so allow them to stand at room temperature for 30 minutes before serving.

Lemon Bars

With a zingy lemony flavor and a crunchy cookie base, these are zesty and refreshing sweet treats everyone will enjoy. Gently dust with confectioners' sugar to sweeten the lemon flavor, or add lemon zest to the topping for an extra lemony taste.

Makes 16 squares

Base
- 1¼ cups (160 g) all-purpose flour
- ¼ cup (50 g) superfine sugar
- ½ cup (120 g) dairy-free butter/margarine

Lemon topping
- ⅔ cup (160 ml) lemon juice (around 3 medium lemons)
- 1 cup plus 1 tablespoon (250 g) coconut cream (see Tip)
- 1¼ cups (250 g) superfine sugar
- 6 tablespoons cornstarch
- ¼ teaspoon ground turmeric or yellow gel food coloring (optional)

- Confectioners' sugar, sifted, to dust

HOLLY'S TIP

You can extract coconut cream from a can of coconut milk. See page 14 for a description of how to do this.

BASE

1. Preheat the oven to 400°F (200°C) and line an 8-inch (20 cm) square baking pan with parchment paper (see page 17 for how to line a cake pan). Allow the paper to hang on either side of the pan so it's easier to remove the bars once baked.

2. Place the flour and superfine sugar in a bowl and combine with a wooden spoon. Rub in the butter or margarine with your fingers until a dough forms.

3. Press the dough into the lined pan, prick with a fork, and pop into the oven to bake for 25–30 minutes, or until golden. Set aside to cool. Leave the oven on, as you will need it later.

LEMON TOPPING

1. Place all of the topping ingredients in a medium saucepan over medium heat. Stir constantly until the mixture thickens (this will take around 5 minutes). Stirring will prevent any sticking and burning, and will remove any lumps.

2. Once the mixture is thick and glossy, remove it from the heat. Spread the topping over the baked base and smooth out with a spoon or spatula—do this immediately, while the topping is still warm, as it will become more difficult as it cools. Place the pan in the oven and bake for 10 minutes.

3. Remove the pan from the oven and allow the bake to cool down to room temperature, then transfer it to the fridge, still in its pan. Leave for 6 hours or overnight. Using the parchment paper, lift the lemon slab out of the pan, dust with some confectioners' sugar, cut into squares, and enjoy.

Store the bars in a sealed container in the fridge and leave at room temperature for 20 minutes before enjoying. Best eaten within a few days.

Rocky Road

The old saying goes that you can never have too much of a good thing, and that is certainly the case with these rocky road bars. Crammed full of chocolate, cookies, marshmallows, and raisins, they don't last long in my house! Perfect for any occasion, they're also especially popular with children. Customize this recipe by adding a sprinkling of your favorite nuts for extra texture and goodness.

Makes 12 squares

- I cup plus 3 tablespoons (200 g) dairy-free white chocolate
- I cup plus 3 tablespoons (200 g) dairy-free dark chocolate
- 2½ tablespoons dairy-free butter/margarine
- 2 tablespoons golden syrup
- 7 ounces (200 g) vegan cookies or graham crackers, broken into small pieces
- ½ cup plus 1½ table-spoons (100 g) raisins
- 1½ cups (100 g) vegan marshmallows or mini marshmallows

1. Line a 9-inch (23 cm) square baking pan with parchment paper (see page 17 for how to line a baking pan). Allow the paper to hang on either side of the pan so it's easier to remove the bars when ready. Melt both types of chocolate with the butter or margarine and the golden syrup using a bain-marie (see page 17). Stir until the mixture is smooth. Remove from the heat and allow to cool for 10 minutes—it shouldn't be too hot, or it could melt the marshmallows.

2. Place the cookies in a large mixing bowl along with the raisins and marshmallows. Pour over the chocolate mixture and stir to combine, but don't overmix.

3. Spoon the mixture into the prepared pan and tap it on the worktop. Make sure to press the mixture down to compact it.

4. Place in the freezer for 1 hour, or until firm. Alternatively, you can refrigerate for at least 2 hours, or until completely firm. Once firm, remove from the pan, cut into squares, and serve.

Enjoy these on the day you make them, or store them in the fridge in a sealed container, where they'll keep for a few weeks.

Chocolate Orange Fridge Fudge

This is not a magic trick—you really can make creamy chocolate orange fudge with only three main ingredients. I prefer to use chocolate with a higher cocoa content for this recipe, as I find it gives the fudge a richer taste. You can use these fudge squares to decorate your baking and dessert creations, or simply store them in the fridge and help yourself to a satisfyingly sweet treat at any time of day.

Makes 12 squares

- 1¾ cups (300 g) dairy-free dark chocolate
- 1 cup (300 g) dairy-free condensed milk
- 1 teaspoon orange extract
- Grated orange zest, to decorate (optional)

1. Line an 8-by-6-inch (20 by 15 cm) rectangular pan with parchment paper (see page 17 for how to line a baking pan). Allow the paper to hang on either side of the pan so it makes it easier to remove the fudge.

2. Place the chocolate and condensed milk in a medium saucepan over medium heat. Mix until the chocolate melts and the mixture is smooth (this will take a few minutes). Turn off the heat. Add the orange extract and stir to combine.

3. Pour the mixture into the lined pan, using a spoon to spread it into the corners and to level it. Sprinkle with the grated orange zest, if using. Place in the fridge overnight to set. Alternatively, you can place it in the freezer for 3–5 hours.

4. When the fudge is fully set, lift it out of the pan, remove the paper, and cut it into squares.

Store in a sealed container in the fridge for up to 2 weeks and help yourself whenever you fancy a treat! Alternatively, store in the freezer wrapped in parchment paper in a sealed container. Thaw for about 1–2 hours in the fridge—less if left out of the fridge.

Speculoos Truffles

My Biscoff recipes are some of the most popular on my blog—my followers absolutely love them. These truffles are ultra-creamy and delicious, with a distinct speculoos flavor. Once you've tried one, you'll struggle to stop coming back for more and more! They're perfect for snacking, sharing with friends, and serving at parties. They also make great gifts and brilliant cake decorations. Use dark chocolate instead of white if that's what you prefer—or, even better, make a batch of both.

Makes 14

- 3 cups (250 g) vegan speculoos cookies (I use Biscoff)
- ½ cup (120 g) dairy-free cream cheese
- 1 cup plus 2 tablespoons (150 g) dairy-free white chocolate
- 1 teaspoon melted coconut oil, if needed
- ½ tablespoon (10 g) vegan speculoos spread (I use Biscoff), melted, to decorate

HOLLY'S TIP

If you don't have a food processor, place the cookies in a plastic zip-top bag and crush them with a rolling pin.

1. Line a baking sheet with parchment paper (see page 17 for how to line a sheet). Place the cookies in a food processor and blend until crumb-like.

2. Place the cookie crumbs in a large mixing bowl and add the cream cheese. Mix them together with a wooden spoon until fully incorporated.

3. With clean hands, roll the mixture between your palms until you have small, truffle-like balls—try to make them equal in size, about 1 level tablespoon (25 g) each. Place the balls on the lined sheet.

4. Pop the sheet into the freezer and leave to set for around 30 minutes.

5. Around 5 minutes before the balls are ready to come out of the freezer, pop the chocolate into a heatproof bowl. You can temper the chocolate if you would like it to set and be firmer (see page 207). Otherwise, melt the chocolate using a bain-marie (see page 17). Add the coconut oil if the chocolate is too thick—it will make it silkier. (You can melt the chocolate in the microwave if you'd prefer.)

6. Once melted, carefully take the saucepan off the heat and place the bowl of chocolate on a heatproof surface. Remove the truffle balls from the freezer and, using a spoon, dip them in the melted chocolate to coat.

7. Place the coated truffles back on the lined sheet. When all the truffles are fully coated, pop the baking sheet back into the freezer for 10–15 minutes until fully set (as the truffles are already cold, the chocolate will set almost immediately).

8. To decorate, dip a spoon into the melted speculoos spread and, using fast motions, zigzag the spread over the truffles, creating decorative lines.

These are best enjoyed at room temperature. If you don't eat them all at once, store in a sealed container in the fridge for up to 2 weeks.

Baked Cookie Dough Cheesecake Bars

Experimenting with ingredients and creating new recipes is a huge passion of mine. For this recipe, I blended two of my favorite sweet treats—cookie dough and cheesecake—and these are the result: deliciously naughty cookie dough cheesecake bars. Smooth and creamy vanilla cheesecake envelops tasty chunks of chocolate chip cookie dough. Are you drooling yet? Because I am!

Makes 12 bars

Base
- 2 cups (180 g) whole or rolled oats
- ⅓ cup plus 1 tablespoon (80 g) superfine sugar
- ⅓ cup plus 1¼ tablespoons (95 g) dairy-free butter/margarine

Cookie dough
- 3½ tablespoons dairy-free butter/margarine, melted
- 2½ tablespoons dark brown sugar
- 1 heaped tablespoon superfine sugar
- 1 tablespoon dairy-free cream
- ½ teaspoon vanilla extract
- ¾ cup plus 1 tablespoon (100 g) all-purpose flour
- ¼ cup (40 g) dairy-free chocolate chips

Filling
- 1¼ cups (150 g) cashews, soaked in water for at least 4 hours or overnight to make them soft, creamy, and easy to blend
- ¾ cup plus 2 tablespoons (200 g) dairy-free cream cheese
- 1 cup plus 1 tablespoon (250 g) silken tofu
- ½ cup (100 g) superfine sugar
- 1 teaspoon vanilla extract
- Dash of dairy-free milk, if needed
- ¼ cup (40 g) dairy-free chocolate chips

BASE

1. Preheat the oven to 400°F (200°C) and line an 8-inch (20 cm) square baking pan with parchment paper (see page 17 for how to line a baking pan). Allow the paper to hang on either side of the pan so it's easier to remove the bars when baked. Place the oats in a food processor or blender and blend until they resemble flour. The result should be very fine, with no lumps. Add the superfine sugar and butter or margarine, and pulse until the mixture comes together.

2. Press the mixture into the lined pan. Set aside.

COOKIE DOUGH

1. Place the melted butter or margarine in a large mixing bowl along with both sugars and combine using a wooden spoon.

2. Add the cream and vanilla and mix together. Fold in the flour until combined. Finally, mix in the chocolate chips. Bring the dough together with your hands, then set aside.

FILLING

1. Drain then rinse the cashews and place them in a food processor or blender along with the cream cheese, tofu, superfine sugar, and vanilla extract. Blend until smooth. Add a dash of milk, if needed, for a creamy consistency.

2. Transfer to a bowl and fold in the chocolate chips. Pour the filling over the base. Tap the pan on the worktop a few times to remove any air bubbles. Push small chunks of the cookie dough into the filling, making sure to use it all up.

Recipe continued on page 140

3. Bake the cheesecake for 40–45 minutes, or until the edges turn golden. The cheesecake will look soft in the middle, but it will firm up as it cools down. Once the cheesecake has baked, allow it to cool fully in the pan, then place it in the fridge to set (I leave mine to set overnight).

4. Once set, carefully remove the cheesecake from the pan, slice into square bars, and enjoy.

Store the cheesecake in a sealed container in the fridge and eat within a few days of making.

Raspberry Crumble Bars

These crumbly and delightfully sweet bars are made with juicy raspberry jam. I've included ground almonds, as they complement the sweet raspberry perfectly and add a delicious texture and flavor. These bars can be made gluten-free by using gluten-free oats and flour. You can customize them for Christmas by using mincemeat and flaked almonds instead of jam. *See photo on page 142.*

Makes 8

- 2¼ cups (200 g) whole or rolled oats
- 3 tablespoons (20 g) ground almonds
- ⅓ cup plus 2½ tablespoons (60 g) all-purpose flour
- ¾ cup (170 g) dairy-free butter/margarine
- 2 tablespoons maple syrup
- 1 tablespoon almond extract
- 3 tablespoons raspberry jam (see page 203 for a homemade version)

1. Preheat the oven to 400°F (200°C) and line an 8-inch (20 cm) square baking pan with parchment paper (see page 17 for how to line a baking pan). Allow the paper to hang on either side of the pan so it makes it easier to remove the bars when baked. Place the oats, ground almonds, and flour in a large mixing bowl.

2. Melt the butter or margarine and the maple syrup together in a small saucepan over medium heat. Pour the melted ingredients into the dry mixture and mix together until combined, then stir in the almond extract.

3. Spoon half of the mixture into the lined baking pan and press down firmly using a spoon, making sure to get right to the edges.

4. Spread the raspberry jam over the top, then top with the other half of the oat mixture and level with a spoon, pressing it down firmly.

5. Pop the pan into the middle of the oven and bake for 20–25 minutes, or until golden brown.

6. Once baked, remove the pan from the oven and place on a cooling rack to cool completely before lifting the crumble out and slicing it into bars.

Keep stored in a sealed container in the fridge. Best enjoyed within a few days of making.

No-Bake Chocolate and Peanut Bars

A Snickers is one of my favorite chocolate bars: nougat, peanuts, caramel, and chocolate—heaven. This is my vegan version, with a peanut base, creamy nut butter filling, even more peanuts, and a dairy-free chocolate coating. If you love peanut butter, you'll be nuts about these bars! Customize the recipe by using gluten-free oats to make it gluten-free.

Makes 16 bars

Base
- 2 cups plus 1 tablespoon (150 g) whole or rolled oats
- 1 cup (150 g) shelled peanuts
- ⅓ cup plus 1 tablespoon (120 g) smooth or crunchy peanut butter
- ½ teaspoon vanilla extract
- 4½ tablespoons coconut oil, melted
- 2 tablespoons maple syrup

Filling
- 1 cup (280 g) smooth or crunchy peanut butter
- ½ cup (80 g) shelled peanuts, whole or chopped (optional)

Chocolate topping
- 1⅓ cups plus 2 tablespoons (250 g) dark chocolate

BASE

1. Line a 9-inch (22 cm) square baking pan with parchment paper (see page 17 for how to line a baking pan). Allow the paper to hang on either side of the pan so it's easy to remove once the bars are ready. In a food processor or blender, blend all of the base ingredients until they come together—this will take a few minutes. Press the mixture into the lined pan, using your hands, until it is compact, smooth, and even.

FILLING

1. Spread the peanut butter over the base and level with a spoon or spatula until even. Sprinkle over the peanuts, if using, and lightly press down. Place the pan in the freezer to allow the peanut butter to firm up. This will take around 15–20 minutes.

CHOCOLATE TOPPING

1. Melt the chocolate using a bain-marie (see page 17) or you can temper the chocolate to make it more stable (see page 207 for how to temper chocolate).

2. Pour this melted chocolate over the filling, level it out with a spoon or spatula, then pop the pan back into the freezer for a few minutes to firm up. Cut into bars just before the chocolate fully sets. Then place the bars in the fridge in a sealed container.

As these bars contain coconut oil, they will soften at room temperature. They can be stored in the fridge for up to a week. Leave at room temperature for 5 minutes before eating.

Gingerbread Cookies

You can't beat the smell of warm gingerbread wafting through the house as a fresh batch of cookies bakes in the oven. A tray of these makes a great gift for friends and family. Have some fun experimenting with differently shaped cookie cutters—snowflakes, reindeer, Christmas trees—the possibilities are endless. You can enjoy these plain or decorate them with vegan royal icing.

Makes around 20 cookies

Cookies
- ⅓ cup (80 g) dairy-free butter/margarine
- 4 tablespoons dark brown sugar
- 1 flax "egg" (see egg replacements, page 15)
- 3 tablespoons black treacle
- 1 teaspoon vanilla extract
- 2 cups plus 1 tablespoon (260 g) all-purpose flour, plus extra for dusting
- 1 teaspoon baking powder
- 2 teaspoons ground ginger
- ½ teaspoon ground cinnamon
- ½ teaspoon ground nutmeg

Decoration
- ¼ batch of royal icing (optional; see page 200)

HOLLY'S TIP
Put some flour on the worktop and coat the bottom of the cutter before each use: this helps to prevent the cutter sticking to the dough.

COOKIES

1. Place the butter or margarine and dark brown sugar in a large mixing bowl and combine—you can use a wooden spoon, an electric hand mixer, or a stand mixer with a paddle attachment. Mix until creamy.

2. Add the flax "egg," black treacle, and vanilla extract and combine. Add the flour, baking powder, and spices and mix until a soft dough forms (you may need to bring it together with your hands).

3. Wrap the dough in parchment paper and let it chill in the fridge for 2 hours before rolling out.

4. Preheat the oven to 400°F (200°C) and line two baking sheets with parchment paper (see page 17 for how to line a baking sheet). Sprinkle flour over a clean worktop. Roll out the chilled dough to a thickness of ¼ inch (5 mm) and cut out the cookies using a medium gingerbread man cutter. You can roll out the dough between two sheets of parchment paper, if you prefer, to prevent any sticking.

5. Place the cookies on the lined baking sheets and bake in the middle of the oven for 10–15 minutes. You may need to bake each sheet separately if there isn't enough room on one rack for both sheets.

6. Once baked, use a spatula to lift up the cookies and place them on a cooling rack. Leave to cool fully before decorating.

7. The royal icing can be made before making the cookies or after. See pages 208–210 for instructions on how to decorate with royal icing.

Store at room temperature in a sealed container or in a cookie jar with a sealed lid—gingerbread cookies can last for months if stored correctly.

CHEESECAKES, TARTS, AND DESSERTS

Sticky Toffee Pudding

The best way to finish off a meal. My recipe has lots of ingredients you'd expect to see in a traditional sticky toffee pudding, with added spices for warmth. Drench it in my rich caramel sauce and dive in!

Serves 9
- ⅔ cup (150 g) dates, pitted
- 2 cups (480 ml) dairy-free milk
- 2 teaspoons apple cider vinegar
- 3⅓ cups plus 1 tablespoon (425 g) self-rising flour
- 2 cups plus 3 tablespoons (440 g) superfine sugar
- 1 teaspoon baking powder
- 1 teaspoon baking soda
- 2 teaspoons ground cinnamon
- 1 teaspoon ground ginger
- ½ cup (120 ml) sunflower oil
- 2 tablespoons black treacle
- 1 cup (245 g) caramel sauce (see page 204)

HOLLY'S TIP

This makes a great second-day pudding—eat it cold or warm it up in the oven or microwave.

1. Preheat the oven to 400°F (200°C) and line a 9-inch (23 cm) deep square baking pan with parchment paper (see page 17 for how to line a cake pan). Place the pitted dates in a bowl of hot water and leave to soak for 20 minutes. Once soaked, drain them and then place them in a food processor or a blender and whizz up until soft and paste-like. Then set aside.

2. In a bowl, whisk the milk with the apple cider vinegar until fully combined. Set aside for 10 minutes to curdle—this creates a vegan buttermilk. In a large mixing bowl, sift the flour, superfine sugar, baking powder, baking soda, cinnamon, and ginger. Mix well to combine.

3. Add the oil to the buttermilk and whisk to combine. Add the buttermilk mixture and the treacle to the dry ingredients and mix. Fold in the dates.

4. Pour the batter into the lined pan. Make sure to tap the pan on the worktop to remove any air bubbles. Place the pan in the center of the oven and bake for 28–30 minutes. You will know it's done when it is springy to the touch and a knife or skewer inserted into the center comes out clean. Remove from the oven and allow to cool in the pan on a cooling rack while you make the caramel sauce.

5. Make a batch of my caramel sauce—see page 204.

6. Allow the sauce to cool slightly before serving, then drizzle over the sponge and enjoy.

Store any leftover sponge in a sealed container in the fridge. Best enjoyed within a few days. You can store the leftover caramel sauce in an airtight container in the fridge for up to a few weeks.

Apple and Blackberry Crumble

This is the perfect dessert for an autumn day. The topping melts in your mouth and is subtly sweet and crunchy, while the fruit offers a delicious tangy contrast. My dad gives it two thumbs up, and he always goes back for second helpings! You can use any oats for this, but if you're making it gluten-free, ensure that the packaging states that the oats are free from gluten. Serve this fruity crumble with a generous scoop of ice cream, a drizzle of custard, or a swirl of whipped cream as the perfect finishing touch.

Serves 4

Crumble
- ¼ cup (60 g) chilled dairy-free butter/margarine, plus extra for greasing
- 1 cup plus 2 tablespoons (100 g) gluten-free whole or rolled oats
- 3 tablespoons light brown sugar

Filling
- 2½ cups (350 g) blackberries (fresh or frozen)
- 2 medium apples, cored and finely sliced
- 1 tablespoon superfine sugar
- 1 tablespoon lemon juice

- Dairy-free cream, ice cream, or custard, to serve (optional)
- Fresh berries, to serve (optional)

CRUMBLE

1. Preheat the oven to 400°F (200°C). Grease four individual 4-inch (10 cm) ovenproof ramekins or a 9-inch (23 cm) pie dish. In a medium mixing bowl, stir together the oats and light brown sugar to combine.

2. Using your fingertips, rub in the butter or margarine until the oats and sugar clump together. Set aside.

FILLING

1. Place the blackberries, sliced apples, superfine sugar, and lemon juice in a bowl and stir to combine.

2. Equally divide the fruity mixture among the ramekins, or simply pour it into the pie dish. Sprinkle the crumble topping over the fruit.

3. Place the ramekins or dish in the center of the oven and bake for 30–40 minutes, or until the fruit mixture is bubbling and the crumble is a golden brown. Remove from the oven and allow to cool slightly. Serve with an optional scoop of cream, ice cream, or custard, and fresh berries.

You can eat the crumble(s) chilled if you prefer, but this dessert is best enjoyed on the day you make it.

Strawberry Trifles

These chilled trifles are the perfect combination of strawberries, custard, and cream, and are unbeatable on a hot summer's day. Make this recipe even simpler by using store-bought dairy-free custard and jam. If using homemade custard and jam, prepare these before you start. For an extra delicious adults-only version, you could soak the sponge in sherry and top with whipped cream and fresh strawberries. *See photo on page 156.*

Serves 4

Sponge layer
- 1 cup (240 ml) dairy-free milk
- 1 teaspoon apple cider vinegar
- 1⅔ cups (210 g) self-rising flour
- ½ cup (100 g) superfine sugar
- ½ teaspoon baking powder
- ½ teaspoon baking soda
- ¼ cup (60 g) sunflower oil

Trifle layers and topping
- Splash of vegan-friendly sherry (optional; ½ to 1 teaspoon depending on your taste)
- 10 large strawberries, 7 sliced and 3 chopped
- ½ cup (115 g) berry jam (see page 203 to make your own)
- 1¼ cups (330 g) dairy-free vanilla custard (see page 190 to make your own)
- 1 cup (100 g) dairy-free whipped cream
- Extra soft fruit, to top (optional)

SPONGE LAYER

1. Preheat the oven to 400°F (200°C) and line a 15-by-10-by-1-inch (38 by 25 by 2.5 cm) baking sheet with parchment paper (see page 17 for how to line a baking pan). In a small bowl, whisk the milk with the apple cider vinegar until fully combined. Set aside for 10 minutes to curdle—this creates a vegan buttermilk.

2. In a large mixing bowl, sift the flour, superfine sugar, baking powder, and baking soda. Mix to combine.

3. Pour the oil into the buttermilk and whisk to combine. Add the wet ingredients to the dry and mix until smooth.

4. Pour the mixture into the lined sheet and level off with a palette knife or spoon. Tap the baking sheet a few times on the worktop to remove any air bubbles.

5. Pop it into the center of the oven and bake for 18–20 minutes. You will know it's done when the sponge is springy to the touch and a knife or skewer inserted into the center comes out clean. Place the pan on a cooling rack and allow the sponge to cool.

TRIFLE LAYERS AND TOPPING

1. You will need four medium serving glasses. Using a cookie cutter a tiny bit smaller than the base of your serving glasses, cut out circles of sponge.

2. Place one sponge into each glass and add a splash of sherry, if using.

3. Add the sliced strawberries to the outer edge of each glass and then spread 1 teaspoon of jam over each sponge circle.

4. Add a generous layer of custard (about 2 tablespoons) to each glass and spread it out to the sides slightly, then sprinkle over some chopped strawberries. Repeat the layers until you reach the top of the glass, finishing with a sponge layer.

5. Top with dairy-free whipped cream, which can be spooned on or decoratively piped. Sprinkle with chopped strawberries and add extra fruit, if you like.

These are best enjoyed on the day you make them.

Mini Passion Fruit Pavlovas

A pavlova is a meringue-based dessert that's crisp on the outside, chewy on the inside, and traditionally topped with fruit. I've used passion fruit in this recipe, as it looks exotic and complements the cream topping perfectly. Such a beautiful dessert to enjoy on a warm summer's day. *See photo on page 157.*

Serves 4

- ¾ cup (170 ml) aquafaba
- ½ teaspoon cream of tartar
- ½ cup plus 1 tablespoon (115 g) superfine sugar
- 4 tablespoons double or thick dairy-free cream
- 4 passion fruit
- Confectioners' sugar, sifted, to dust (optional)

HOLLY'S TIP

Customize it— use a different fruit if you prefer.

1. Preheat the oven to 275°F (140°C) and line a baking sheet with parchment paper (see page 17 for how to line a baking sheet).

2. Place the aquafaba in a small saucepan over medium heat. Simmer until it reduces by about half to roughly ⅓ cup (85 ml), which will take about 5–10 minutes.

3. Once reduced, place the aquafaba in a mixing bowl and, using an electric mixer, whizz it up on high until it is fluffy and is holding soft peaks (this will take around 5 minutes). I prefer to use my stand mixer with a balloon-whisk attachment, but you can use an electric hand mixer. Once fluffy, add the cream of tartar.

4. Still mixing on high speed, add the superfine sugar a little at a time. You may need to scrape the mixture down from the sides of the bowl a few times to ensure it's all incorporated. After about 10–15 minutes, the mixture will turn thick and glossy. To check if it's ready, rub some mixture between your fingers: if it feels gritty, it needs more time.

5. When ready, spoon 4 dollops of meringue onto the lined sheet, using approximately 2 heaped dessertspoons for each one and making sure they're equal in size. Use the back of a spoon or a small spatula to help mold the meringues into 3-inch (7½ cm) rounds about 1 inch (2½ cm) in height. Leave space in between them because they will spread out.

HOLLY'S TIP

To make sure they are all the same shape and size, you can draw circles in pencil on the parchment paper and turn it over, leaving a stencil.

6. Place the baking sheet in the bottom of the oven and bake for 70 minutes, or until the meringues are dry to the touch. Meringues don't like sudden changes in temperature, so once they're baked, turn off the oven and allow them to cool down fully on the sheet in the oven. This will also help dry them out. This will take around 2 hours.

7. Top with the cream and fruit just before serving (and not before; otherwise, they'll become soggy)—add a tablespoon of whipped cream on top of each meringue, followed by a tablespoon of fresh passion fruit. Dust with confectioners' sugar, if using.

Once they are cold, the meringues can be stored in a sealed container in the fridge until you want to serve them. These are best served on the day you make them. The meringues will soften the longer they are kept.

Lemon Meringue Pie

This is my vegan take on a popular classic with a pastry base, zesty lemon curd filling, and sweet meringue topping. Looks stunning and is timeless!

Serves 10

Base
- ⅓ cup plus 2 tablespoons (100 g) coconut oil, melted, plus extra for greasing
- 2 cups (250 g) all-purpose flour
- 3 tablespoons maple syrup

Lemon curd filling
- 6–7 medium lemons
- 1½ cups plus 1½ tablespoons (320 g) superfine sugar
- ½ cup plus 1½ tablespoons (90 g) cornstarch
- Pinch of ground turmeric (optional)
- 2 tablespoons dairy-free butter/margarine

Meringue
- ⅓ cup plus 1½ tablespoons (100 ml) aquafaba
- ½ cup (100 g) superfine sugar
- 2 teaspoons cream of tartar
- ½ teaspoon vanilla bean paste or vanilla extract

HOLLY'S TIP

Make the meringue topping on the day you're serving the pie. It will help it stay fresh and crisp.

BASE

1. Preheat the oven to 400°F (200°C) and lightly grease a 9-inch (23 cm) removable-bottom fluted tart pan with coconut oil. In a mixing bowl, combine the flour, maple syrup, and melted coconut oil. Mix and bring together with your hands until a dough forms.

2. Using your fingers, press the dough into the greased pan, making sure to get it into the fluted sides. Trim the top edges using a knife. Prick the base with a fork and pop into the center of the oven for 12–15 minutes, or until golden. Remove from the oven and lightly press down the base. Allow to cool in the pan before filling.

LEMON CURD FILLING

1. Zest 1 lemon and juice all of the lemons until you get 1 cup (240 ml) of juice. Place the zest and juice, superfine sugar, cornstarch, and turmeric, if using, in a medium saucepan. Heat over medium-high heat and, using a hand mixer, stir constantly to prevent from burning and sticking to the pan. The mixture will thicken and become translucent; this will take around 5–10 minutes.

2. Once the curd has thickened, remove from the heat and mix in the butter or margarine. Leave it for a few minutes to cool slightly. Then spread it over the base while it's still warm. Leave to cool fully in the pan, then chill it in the fridge for a few hours before adding the meringue topping (see Tip).

MERINGUE

1. Using a stand mixer or food processor, whip the aquafaba on high speed until it is fluffy and holds soft peaks; this will take around 5 minutes.

2. On low speed, gradually add in the superfine sugar, cream of tartar, and vanilla paste or extract. Turn the speed to high and keep going until stiff peaks form; you may need to scrape down the sides of the bowl. It will take around 5 minutes for the mixture to turn into a glossy, thick meringue.

THE ESSENTIAL BOOK OF VEGAN BAKES

3. Spoon the meringue on top of the lemon filling and create peaks with a spoon or fork. Toast the meringue using a blowtorch or under the broiler until golden, being careful not to burn it.

This pie is best served on the day you make it, but can be kept in a sealed container in the fridge (see Tip on page 160).

Cherry Bakewell Tartlets

These cherry Bakewell tartlets were a must to include in this book, as they are my dad's ultimate dessert. I use my simple three-ingredient base and top it with spongy frangipane, which has notes of nutty almond and cherry jam, then drizzle it with almond icing. *See photo on page 164.*

Makes 6 tartlets

Base
- ½ cup plus 1 tablespoon (125 g) coconut oil, melted, plus extra for greasing (optional)
- 1¾ cups (220 g) all-purpose flour
- 4 tablespoons maple syrup

Jam filling
- 1 cup (340 g) cherry jam

Frangipane
- ⅓ cup (65 g) superfine sugar
- 3 tablespoons coconut oil, melted
- ¼ cup (30 g) all-purpose flour
- 3 tablespoons dairy-free milk
- 1 teaspoon cornstarch
- 3 teaspoons almond extract
- ½ teaspoon baking powder
- 1 cup (100 g) ground almonds
- Flaked almonds (optional)

Icing
- ½ cup (60 g) confectioners' sugar, sifted
- 1 teaspoon almond extract
- 2 teaspoons water

- Fresh cherries, to decorate (optional)

BASE

1. Preheat the oven to 400°F (200°C) and lightly grease six 4-inch (10 cm) mini removable-bottom tartlet pans with coconut oil. (It's best to grease fluted pans.)

2. In a mixing bowl, combine the flour, maple syrup, and melted coconut oil. Mix and bring together with your hands until a dough forms. If it's too wet, add more flour; if it's too dry, add more oil—you want it to feel like pastry dough.

3. Using your fingers, press the dough into the pans—it shouldn't be too thick or too thin. Repeat for all of the tartlets, then prick the bases with a fork a few times.

4. Prebake the bases by placing them in the center of the oven to bake for around 4 minutes. Allow to cool fully before filling.

5. Spread approximately 2 teaspoons of cherry jam onto each cooled base.

FRANGIPANE

1. In a large mixing bowl, combine the superfine sugar and melted coconut oil. Add the flour, milk, cornstarch, almond extract, and baking powder. Mix with a wooden spoon to combine.

2. Fold in the ground almonds until fully incorporated (the mixture will be quite thick and sticky). Spread approximately 2 tablespoons of frangipane on top of the jam in each tartlet. I find it helpful to use a small fork to spread the mixture out evenly. If using, scatter flaked almonds over each tartlet.

3. Bake the tartlets for 25–30 minutes, or until they are golden brown and the frangipane is slightly springy. Check after 20 minutes because you don't want the bases to burn. To prevent this, you can lightly cover the tartlets with foil.

4. Once the tartlets have baked, remove them from the oven and allow them to cool in their pans before icing.

ICING

1. Put the confectioners' sugar and almond extract in a bowl and mix. Stir in the water, a teaspoon at a time, until it reaches a drizzle consistency.

2. When the tartlets have fully cooled, remove them from their pans and drizzle with the icing. Decorate with fresh cherries, if you like.

These are best served on the day you make them, though they can be stored in a sealed container for 1–2 days in the fridge. Leave at room temperature for 20–30 minutes before serving.

Salted Caramel Tartlets

Indulge in these mini tarts with a crumbly chocolate crust; a rich and smooth dark chocolate ganache filling; and a silky, sweet caramel sauce with an added sprinkle of salt. Sound amazing? They truly are, and they would be great to serve up at a dinner party. For convenience, make the sauce the day before—this will also give it time to thicken! *See photo on page 165.*

Makes 6

- 1 cup (245 g) caramel sauce (see page 204)

Base
- ½ cup (120 g) coconut oil, melted, plus extra for greasing
- 1⅔ cups (200 g) all-purpose flour
- 2 tablespoons cocoa powder
- 3 tablespoons maple syrup

Chocolate filling
- 1 cup plus 3 tablespoons (200 g) dairy-free dark chocolate chips
- ½ cup (120 g) coconut cream (see Tip)

- Pinch of salt

HOLLY'S TIP
You can extract coconut cream from a can of coconut milk. See page 14 for a description of how to do this.

1. Make the caramel sauce and put it aside to cool.

BASE

1. Preheat the oven to 400°F (200°C) and lightly grease six 4-inch (10 cm) mini removable-bottom tartlet pans with coconut oil.

2. In a mixing bowl, combine the flour, cocoa powder, maple syrup, and melted coconut oil with a wooden spoon until a dough forms.

3. Using your fingers, press the dough into the pans to make bases about ¼ inch (5 mm) thick, then prick the bases with a fork and bake in the center of the oven for 9–10 minutes. Remove from the oven and place them on a cooling rack in their pans. When cool enough to handle, gently remove the bases from the pans, being careful not to break them. Leave to cool fully before filling.

CHOCOLATE FILLING

1. Place the chocolate and coconut cream in a medium saucepan over medium heat and simmer, stirring continuously, until the chocolate has melted and the mixture is smooth and glossy.

2. Evenly distribute the chocolate filling among the tartlets. Once filled, place them in the fridge to set for a few hours.

3. Once set, drizzle a tablespoon of the caramel sauce on top of each tartlet You can save leftover caramel sauce in a sealed container in the fridge for a few weeks. Finish them off with a sprinkling of salt.

These are best eaten within a few days of making. Store in a sealed container in the fridge. Leave at room temperature for 20–30 minutes before serving.

Chocolate Caramel Brownie Cups

At first glance, these look like chocolate cupcakes, but they're actually a fun take on a brownie with a silky chocolate frosting and a drizzle of salted caramel sauce—see the photo on page 4.

Makes 8–9, depending on the pan

Brownie cups
- ½ cup (120 g) dairy-free butter/margarine, plus extra for greasing
- 2 tablespoons milled flaxseed/linseed
- 2 tablespoons water
- ¼ cup (40 g) dairy-free dark chocolate
- ⅓ cup plus 1 tablespoon (60 g) cocoa powder
- ¾ cup plus 1½ table-spoons (160 g) superfine sugar
- 1 teaspoon vanilla extract
- ¾ teaspoon baking powder
- 1 cup (120 g) all-purpose flour
- 2 tablespoons (20 g) dark chocolate drops, for topping

Chocolate frosting
- ⅓ cup plus 2 tablespoons (80 g) dairy-free dark chocolate
- ⅓ cup (80 g) dairy-free block butter (not margarine)
- 3 tablespoons (40 ml) aquafaba
- ⅔ cup (80 g) confectioners' sugar, sifted

- 1 batch of caramel sauce (see page 204)

BROWNIE CUPS

1. Preheat oven to 375°F (190°C). Grease the inside of an extra-deep removable-bottom muffin pan or a cookie cup pan with dairy-free butter or margarine. Line the sides of the cups with parchment paper or muffin liners.

2. Mix the flaxseed/linseed in the water and set aside for 10 minutes. Melt the chocolate and butter or margarine in a small saucepan over low heat, stirring continuously until melted. Add to a medium mixing bowl with the flaxseed mixture, cocoa powder, superfine sugar, vanilla extract, and baking powder.

3. Stir with a wooden spoon or spatula for 1–2 minutes until fully incorporated. Sift in the flour and fold in until a thick brownie mixture forms.

4. Make heaping 3-tablespoon (85 g) balls of the brownie mixture, or 2 tablespoons (60 g) if using a cupcake pan, and place each in a lined cup. Level off by pressing down with your fingertips. Sprinkle over the chocolate drops and lightly press them into the brownie mixture. You can use a toothpick to do this.

5. Place the pan in the center of the oven and bake for 15 minutes. Leave to cool fully in the pan before frosting.

CHOCOLATE FROSTING

1. Melt the chocolate using a bain-marie (see page 17) or in a microwave. Place to one side. Put the butter in a stand mixer or use an electric hand mixer and whip until creamy.

2. Add the melted chocolate and aquafaba to the butter, then add the confectioners' sugar and whip until thick, creamy, and smooth. Transfer to a piping bag fitted with an open star-tip nozzle, or use a spoon. Pipe a swirl of frosting onto each brownie cup and drizzle over as much caramel sauce as you like!

Store in a sealed container in or out of the fridge and eat within 2 days of making. Leave at room temperature for 30 minutes before serving.

American-Style Pancakes

Although both are called pancakes, the American and English versions are really quite different. American pancakes are small and fluffy, perfect for stacking into a pancake tower and drizzling with maple syrup, whereas English pancakes are larger and thinner, more similar to French crêpes. Stack these American-style pancakes and get creative with your toppings—the perfect treat for brunch.

Makes 12 pancakes

- 2 cups (250 g) all-purpose flour
- 1½ tablespoons baking powder
- 2 tablespoons superfine sugar
- Pinch of salt
- 1¼ cups (300 ml) dairy-free milk
- 3 tablespoons sunflower oil, plus extra for frying

Serving suggestions
- Dairy-free cream, butter, or ice cream
- Maple syrup
- Berries
- Jam
- Lemon juice
- Caramel sauce (see page 204)
- Sugar

1. In a bowl, mix together the flour, baking powder, superfine sugar, and salt using a hand mixer. Pour in the milk and oil and combine until smooth. Set aside for 5 minutes.

2. Heat ½ tablespoon of oil in a nonstick frying pan over medium-high heat. When hot, spoon about 2 tablespoons of batter into the pan. Allow the edges of the pancake to turn golden, then flip. It will take around 40 seconds on each side. Once both sides are golden, set the pancake aside somewhere warm while you cook the remaining pancakes. Serve with some dairy-free cream, butter, or ice cream; maple syrup; or whatever toppings you prefer.

They're best eaten hot!

HOLLY'S TIP

You may need to add more oil to the frying pan as you go.

Chocolate Mousse Pots

It only takes three ingredients to create these simple yet indulgent chocolate mousse pots. I love how the chocolate melts in your mouth with every spoonful, and sometimes I like to go all out and top them with chocolate shavings, chopped fruit, or a dollop of whipped dairy-free cream.

Makes 4

- ½ cup (120 ml) aquafaba
- 1 tablespoon superfine sugar
- ½ cup plus 1½ tablespoons (100 g) dairy-free chocolate chips (at least 70% cocoa content)

HOLLY'S TIP

Aquafaba works best at room temperature.

1. Place the aquafaba in a medium mixing bowl along with the superfine sugar and whip together using an electric hand mixer or a stand mixer with a balloon-whisk attachment. (You can do it by hand, but it will take longer.) It will turn foamy at first, but after about 5 minutes of whipping on high, it will start to form stiff peaks. It will be ready when it's thick and glossy.

2. Melt the chocolate using a bain-marie (see page 17) or in the microwave. Place a third of the whipped aquafaba mixture in a separate bowl, then pour in all of the melted chocolate. Whisk the melted chocolate and whipped aquafaba mixture together until fully combined.

3. Add the remaining whipped aquafaba mixture to the bowl and carefully fold everything together with a spatula. Be very gentle when folding the mixture, as you want to keep as much air in the mousse as possible.

4. Once the mousse is smooth, divide it among four 3-inch (7½ cm) ramekins, serving glasses, or similar vessels. The mousse should be thick but easy to pour. Place the desserts in the fridge for a minimum of 5 hours or overnight to set.

Store in the fridge. These are best eaten within 2 days of making.

Key Lime Pie

Key lime pie is made using a type of lime from Florida that is famous for being more aromatic and tart than others. The good news is that you can use any type of lime to make this pie, and my simple two-ingredient base is perfectly paired with the zesty, creamy lime filling. I love to go all out and decorate it with slices of lime and whipped cream. You can make this gluten-free by using gluten-free cookies.

Serves 12

Base
- ⅔ cup (150 g) dairy-free butter/margarine, melted, plus extra for greasing
- 10½ ounces (300 g) vegan cookies or graham crackers

Filling
- 1¼ cups (150 g) cashews, soaked in water for at least 4 hours or overnight to make them soft, creamy, and easy to blend
- ⅔ cup (150 g) coconut cream (see Tip)
- ¾ cup plus 2 tablespoons (200 g) dairy-free cream cheese
- 1 tablespoon superfine sugar
- 3 tablespoons lime juice
- 3 tablespoons lime zest
- 5 spinach leaves (optional)

- Dairy-free whipped cream, to serve
- Lime slices and zest, to serve

HOLLY'S TIP

You can extract coconut cream from a can of coconut milk. See page 14 for a description of how to do this.

BASE

1. Preheat the oven to 400°F (200°C) and grease a 10-inch (25 cm) removable-bottom fluted pie pan with butter or margarine. Place the cookies in a food processor and whizz until crumb-like. Pour the melted butter or margarine into the whizzed-up cookies. Blend until the mixture is like wet sand (you can do this by hand, but it will take longer).

2. Firmly press the cookie mixture into the greased pan and up the sides, making sure it's compacted—I find using my knuckles really helps! Place in the center of the oven and bake for 10 minutes, or until golden. Remove from the oven and set aside to cool.

FILLING

1. Drain and rinse the cashews and place them in a food processor or high-speed blender along with the coconut cream and cream cheese.

2. Add the superfine sugar, lime juice, and zest to the blender along with the spinach leaves, if using (spinach adds a green color to the filling). Blend until smooth. You may need to scrape down the sides of the blender a few times to make sure everything is fully incorporated.

3. Pour the filling onto the cooled base. Spread it out with a spoon or spatula until smooth. Gently tap the pan on the worktop a few times to remove any air bubbles. Place in the freezer for an hour, then in the fridge for at least 2–4 hours or overnight to set.

4. For the cream swirls, put the whipped cream in a piping bag fitted with an open star-tip nozzle and pipe swirls on top of the pie. Add fresh lime slices and a sprinkle of lime zest.

Keep in a sealed container in the fridge. This is best eaten within a few days.

THE ESSENTIAL BOOK OF VEGAN BAKES

Chocolate Orange Tart

This is a super-rich and creamy chocolate tart with an orange flavor and a scrumptious oaty base, guaranteed to be a hit with dinner party guests. I prefer to use dark chocolate, but you can use dairy-free milk chocolate too, and the base uses oat flour, so it's completely gluten-free (provided your oats are gluten-free).

Serves 12

Base
- ½ cup (120 g) coconut oil, melted, plus extra for greasing
- 3½ cups (300 g) gluten-free whole or rolled oats
- 2 tablespoons maple syrup
- 1 teaspoon vanilla extract

Filling
- 1 cup plus 3 tablespoons (200 g) dairy-free dark chocolate
- 1 teaspoon orange extract
- 1⅓ cups plus 2 tablespoons (360 g) silken tofu
- 1 medium orange, zest and juice

Ganache
- ½ cup plus 1½ tablespoons (100 g) dairy-free dark chocolate
- ⅓ cup plus 1½ tablespoons (100 g) dairy-free cream

- Orange zest, grated, to decorate
- Dairy-free chocolate, grated, to decorate
- Orange segments, to decorate (optional)

BASE

1. Preheat the oven to 400°F (200°C) and lightly grease a 9-inch (23 cm) removable-bottom fluted pie pan.

2. To make the oat flour, place the oats in a blender or food processor and whizz up until fine.

3. In a mixing bowl, combine the oat flour, maple syrup, vanilla extract, and melted coconut oil. Mix with a wooden spoon, then bring together with your hands until you can press the mixture together and it sticks.

4. Press the oat dough into the greased pan, pressing it all the way up the sides. You can use your hands to do this. Prick the base with a fork and pop into the oven to bake for 9–10 minutes, or until golden. Remove from the oven and leave to cool in the pan on a cooling rack.

FILLING

1. Melt the chocolate with the orange extract using a bain-marie (see page 17) or in the microwave. Carefully take it off the heat and put aside.

2. Drain the tofu and place it in a blender or food processor along with the melted chocolate, orange zest, and juice. Blend until fully combined and creamy—this will take around 3–4 minutes on high speed. You might need to scrape down the sides of the blender a few times, as the mixture is quite thick, making it harder to blend.

3. Pour the filling into the cooled tart base and smooth out with a spoon or spatula. Place the tart in the fridge for around 4 hours, or until set (I like to leave mine in the fridge overnight to set fully). Once set, remove the tart from the pan and place on a serving plate.

Recipe continued on page 176

GANACHE

You want to add the ganache to the tart when the ganache is still warm, as it's harder to spread when it's cool.

1. Place the chocolate and cream in a medium saucepan over medium heat and simmer, stirring continuously, until the chocolate has melted and is glossy.

2. Pour the warm ganache over the filling and smooth out. Place the tart in the fridge to set the ganache—this will take around 30 minutes. I serve my tart with gratings of orange zest and dairy-free dark chocolate along with a few orange segments.

Store in a sealed container in the fridge and eat within a few days. Leave at room temperature for 20 minutes before serving.

S'mores Glasses

I've transformed this delicious campfire treat into a gorgeous vegan dessert with a cookie base, rich chocolate ganache filling, and creamy meringue topping. Toast the meringue to add an authentic burnt-sugar flavor and light crunch. These are super simple to make and will delight your friends and family. This recipe can be made gluten-free by using gluten-free cookies. *See photo on page 179.*

Serves 6

Base
- 5 ounces (150 g; around 10) vegan graham crackers
- ⅓ cup plus 1 tablespoon (100 g) dairy-free butter/margarine, melted

Chocolate ganache filling
- 1 cup plus 3 tablespoons (200 g) dairy-free dark chocolate chips or broken-up chunks
- 1 cup (220 g) dairy-free cream
- 1 tablespoon maple syrup (optional)

Meringue topping
- 3½ tablespoons (50 ml) aquafaba
- ⅓ cup (70 g) superfine sugar
- 1 teaspoon cream of tartar
- ½ teaspoon vanilla bean paste or vanilla extract

BASE

1. You will need 6 small serving glasses (make sure to use sturdy serving glasses, as regular drinking glasses can be too brittle).

2. Place the graham crackers in a food processor or blender and pulse until crumb-like. (If you don't have a food processor or blender, place the graham crackers in a plastic zip-top bag and crush them with a rolling pin.) Transfer the crumbs to a heatproof dish.

3. Pour the melted butter or margarine over the crumbs and stir with a wooden spoon until the mixture resembles wet sand.

4. Add 2 heaped tablespoons of graham cracker mixture to the bottom of each glass and lightly press down. You don't want to make it too compact; otherwise, it'll be harder to cut into. You can use a spoon or the tips of your fingers.

CHOCOLATE GANACHE FILLING

1. Place the chocolate, cream, and maple syrup, if using, in a medium saucepan over medium heat and simmer, stirring continuously, until the chocolate has melted and is glossy.

2. Add 3½ heaped tablespoons of the chocolate ganache filling to each of the serving glasses. Place the glasses in the fridge for 1 hour to set.

Recipe continued on page 178

MERINGUE TOPPING

1. Using a stand mixer or food processor, whip the aquafaba on high speed until it is fluffy and holds soft peaks. This will take around 5 minutes.

2. On low speed, gradually add in the superfine sugar, cream of tartar, and vanilla paste or extract. Turn the speed back to high and keep going until stiff peaks form; you may need to scrape down the sides of the bowl as you go. It will take around 5 minutes for the mixture to turn into a glossy, thick meringue.

3. Transfer the meringue to a piping bag fitted with an open star-tip nozzle and pipe a swirl of meringue on top of the ganache. If you don't have a piping bag, you can spoon it on.

4. Use a blowtorch to lightly toast the meringue. If you don't have a blowtorch, you can leave them as they are. Top with a sprinkle of graham cracker crumbs.

Store in the fridge and leave at room temperature for about 15 minutes before serving. These are best eaten on the day you make them. Alternatively, you can make the base and filling the day before and add the meringue topping on the day you serve them.

Baked New York Cheesecake

Take a bite of this classic New York cheesecake, then close your eyes and imagine you're sitting in the window of a bustling Manhattan bakery. New York cheesecakes are famous for being dense, smooth, and creamy—one slice goes a long way! Enjoy the deep and ultra-silky filling, which contrasts perfectly with the oaty base. Drizzle on some thick dairy-free cream and fresh berries for extra indulgence. You can make this gluten-free by using gluten-free oats.

Serves 12

Base
- 2 cups (180 g) whole or rolled oats
- ⅓ cup plus 1 tablespoon (80 g) superfine sugar
- ⅓ cup (80 g) dairy-free butter/margarine

Filling
- 2½ cups (300 g) cashews, soaked in water for at least 4 hours or overnight to make them soft, creamy, and easy to blend
- 1¾ cups (400 g) dairy-free cream cheese
- 2 cups plus 1 tablespoon (500 g) silken tofu
- 1 cup (200 g) superfine sugar
- 1 teaspoon vanilla extract

- Dairy-free cream and fresh berries, to serve

BASE

1. Preheat the oven to 400°F (200°C) and line an 8-inch (20 cm) round, removable-bottom, deep cake pan with parchment paper (see page 17 for how to line a cake pan). Place the oats in a food processor and blend until they form a flour. It should be very fine with no lumps.

2. Add the superfine sugar and butter or margarine, and pulse until the mixture comes together. Using a measuring cup or your fingers, press this into the lined cake pan, making sure it's compacted. Set aside.

FILLING

1. Drain and rinse the cashews and place them in a food processor or blender along with the cream cheese, tofu, superfine sugar, and vanilla extract. Blend until smooth.

2. Pour the filling over the crust. Tap the pan on the worktop a few times to remove any air bubbles and to level it out. Bake in the center of the preheated oven for 45–50 minutes, or until the edges of the cheesecake turn golden (check after 45 minutes). The cheesecake will look soft in the middle, but it will firm up as it cools.

3. Once the cheesecake is baked, allow it to cool fully and then place it in the fridge overnight to set fully. Once set, carefully remove the cheesecake from the pan, then slice and serve with whatever dairy-free cream and fresh berries you prefer.

Store in a sealed container in the fridge. This is best enjoyed within a few days of making.

No-Bake Strawberry Cheesecake

Fresh strawberries and cream taste even better when they come in cheesecake form! I've created my no-bake strawberry cheesecake with a crunchy cookie base and filled it with a delicious strawberry cream filling. This is what dessert dreams are made of.

Serves 12

Base
- ⅓ cup (80 g) dairy-free butter or margarine, plus extra for greasing
- 5½ ounces (160 g) vegan cookies or graham crackers

Filling
- 1½ cups (300 g) strawberries
- 3 tablespoons superfine sugar
- 1⅔ cups (200 g) cashews, soaked in water for at least 4 hours or overnight to make them soft, creamy, and easy to blend
- ¾ cup plus 1½ tablespoons (200 g) coconut cream (see Tip)
- 1 cup plus 2 tablespoons (250 g) dairy-free cream cheese
- 2⅓ cups (270 ml) dairy-free whipped cream, to decorate
- 4 strawberries, halved, to decorate
- 2 vegan cookies, crushed, to decorate

HOLLY'S TIP

You can extract coconut cream from a can of coconut milk. See page 14 for a description of how to do this.

BASE

1. Grease an 8-inch (20 cm) round, removable-bottom, deep cake pan with butter or margarine. Place the cookies in a blender or food processor and blend until crumb-like. If you don't have a blender or food processor, place them into a plastic zip-top bag and crush them with a rolling pin. Melt the butter or margarine in a saucepan over low heat. Place the cookie crumbs into a heatproof bowl, pour over the melted butter or margarine, and stir together until it's like wet sand.

2. Using a measuring cup or your fingers, press the mixture into the greased cake pan, making sure it's compacted. Place the base in the fridge while you make the filling.

FILLING

1. Make a strawberry purée by placing the strawberries and superfine sugar in a pan. Place over medium heat and crush the strawberries with a potato masher. Stir with a wooden spoon until the mixture has reduced by about one-third. This will take about 10–12 minutes. Set aside to cool fully.

2. Drain and rinse the cashews and place into a food processor or blender along with the coconut cream, dairy-free cream cheese, and strawberry purée. Blend on high for around 4–5 minutes until it's smooth and creamy. You may have to scrape down the sides of the blender a few times to make sure everything gets fully blended.

3. Pour the cheesecake mixture over the base. Place it into the freezer for 2 hours and then place it in the fridge for 4–6 hours or overnight to set.

4. Decorate just before serving—add some whipped cream into a piping bag fitted with an open star-tip nozzle and pipe swirls on the top edge of the cheesecake. Decorate with the strawberry halves and cookie crumbs.

Store in the fridge in a sealed container; best eaten within 2 days.

No-Bake Gingerbread Cheesecake

Gingerbread evokes warm and fuzzy festive feelings deep in my heart. I love nothing more than a festive fix of gingerbread, whether that be a gingerbread latte or a generous serving of my gingerbread cheesecake! Of course, this cheesecake can be enjoyed year-round, with its ginger-spiced crunchy base and a super-smooth filling topped with whipped cream swirls and gingersnap crumbs. Remember to add the whipped cream just before you serve so it's at its freshest!

Serves 12

Base
- ⅓ cup plus 1¼ table-spoons (95 g) dairy-free butter/margarine, melted, plus extra for greasing
- 30 vegan gingersnaps (300 g)

Filling
- 2 cups plus 2 tablespoons (250 g) cashews, soaked in water for at least 4 hours or overnight to make them soft, creamy, and easy to blend
- 1¼ cup (300 g) coconut cream (see Tip on page 183)
- 1⅓ cups (300 g) dairy-free cream cheese
- 10 vegan gingersnaps (100 g)
- 1½ teaspoons vanilla extract

- Dairy-free whipped cream, to decorate (optional)
- Vegan gingersnap crumbs, to decorate (optional)

BASE

1. Grease an 8-inch (20 cm) round, removable-bottom, deep cake pan with butter or margarine. Place the gingersnaps in a blender or food processor and blend until crumb-like. If you don't have a blender or food processor, place them in a plastic zip-top bag and crush them with a rolling pin.

2. Put the crushed gingersnaps in a bowl and pour over the melted butter or margarine. Mix until it resembles wet sand. Using a measuring cup or your fingers, press the mixture into the lined pan and up the sides, making sure it's compacted (this will help prevent it from crumbling when removing it from the pan). Add a little more melted butter or margarine if the gingersnap base is too crumbly. Place the pan in the fridge while you make the filling.

FILLING

1. Drain and rinse the cashews and place them in a food processor or blender along with the coconut cream, cream cheese, gingersnaps, and vanilla extract. Blend until smooth and creamy—you may have to scrape down the sides of the blender a few times to make sure everything gets fully incorporated.

2. Pour the filling over the base and level with a spoon or spatula. Tap the pan on the worktop a few times to remove any air bubbles. Place the cheesecake in the freezer for 2 hours and then in the fridge for 4–6 hours or overnight to set. Decorate just before serving with whipped cream stars and crumbled gingersnaps, if using.

Store in a sealed container in the fridge; best eaten within 2 days.

No-Bake Speculoos Cheesecake

You'll be in heaven with this dreamy cheesecake. This is one of the most popular recipes on my blog and has been enjoyed by many of my followers. I have tweaked it for this book. If you love speculoos as much as I do, you can add crushed speculoos cookies to the filling as well—how incredible does that sound?! You could also replace the speculoos with any cookies of your choice—have fun with flavors!

Serves 12

Base
- ⅓ cup plus 1¼ table-spoons (95 g) dairy-free butter/margarine, plus extra for greasing
- 30 (230 g) vegan speculoos cookies (I use Biscoff)

Filling
- 2 cups plus 2 tablespoons (250 g) cashews, soaked in water for 4 hours or overnight to make them soft, creamy, and easy to blend
- 1¼ cups (300 g) coconut cream (see Tip)
- 1 cup plus 2 tablespoons (250 g) dairy-free cream cheese
- ½ cup (150 g) smooth vegan speculoos spread (I use Biscoff)

Topping
- ¼ cup (80 g) smooth vegan speculoos spread
- 2 vegan speculoos cookies, crushed

HOLLY'S TIP

You can extract coconut cream from a can of coconut milk. See page 14 for a description of how to do this.

BASE

1. Grease an 8-inch (20 cm) round, removable-bottom, shallow cake pan with butter or margarine. Place the cookies in a food processor or blender and whizz up until crumbly but not too fine. If you don't have a food processor or blender, place them into a plastic zip-top bag and crush them with a rolling pin. Melt the butter or margarine in a saucepan over low heat.

2. Place the crushed cookies in a bowl and pour over the melted butter or margarine. Mix until it resembles wet sand. Using a measuring cup or your fingers, press the mixture into the greased cake pan, making sure it's compacted. Place in the freezer while you make the filling.

FILLING AND TOPPING

1. Drain and rinse the cashews and place them in a food processor or blender along with the coconut cream, cream cheese, and speculoos spread. Whizz up on high for around 5 minutes until smooth.

2. Pour the filling over the base and level with a spoon. Tap the pan on the worktop a few times to remove any air bubbles. Pop into the freezer for at least 2 hours, then place it in the fridge for 4–6 hours or overnight to set.

3. Decorate the cheesecake just before serving. Melt the speculoos spread using a bain-marie (see page 17) or in the microwave, then spread it over the cheesecake using an offset spatula or palette knife. Sprinkle the crushed cookies on the outer edge of the cheesecake. Leave it to set slightly before serving.

Store in a sealed container in the fridge. Best eaten within 2 days.

BASICS

Vanilla Custard

Custard traditionally contains dairy milk and egg yolks, but my custard recipe has swapped those out for simple vegan ingredients—and it tastes incredible! In very little time, you'll be able to create deliciously creamy custard that everyone will love. I recommend using a blender for the best results.

Makes 1¼ cups (330 g)

- 1¼ cups (300 g) silken tofu
- ⅓ cup plus ½ tablespoon (70 g) superfine sugar
- ½ cup plus 1 tablespoon (130 g) coconut cream (see Tip)
- 1 teaspoon nutritional yeast
- 1 teaspoon vanilla extract
- 1 tablespoon cornstarch

HOLLY'S TIP

You can extract coconut cream from a can of coconut milk. See page 14 for a description of how to do this.

HOLLY'S TIP

To make chocolate custard, simply add 3 tablespoons of cocoa powder to the blender along with the rest of the ingredients.

1. Drain the excess water from the silken tofu, then place the tofu and the remaining ingredients for the custard in a high-speed blender and blend until smooth.

2. Pour the custard into a medium saucepan and place over medium heat, whisking constantly as it starts to thicken—this will take around 3–6 minutes.

3. When the custard has thickened, remove the pan from the heat and serve (if you want to serve it hot). Otherwise, to cool it down quickly to serve cold, place the bottom of the pan into an ice bath (a bowl of ice and cold water)—just make sure no water gets into the custard! Whisk the custard as it cools down in the ice bath to prevent it from clumping and forming a skin.

4. When the custard has cooled, transfer it to a sealed container. It can be stored in the fridge for a few days.

You can heat it up, enjoy it cold with your favorite dessert, or use it in my strawberry trifles recipe on page 154.

American-Style Vanilla Buttercream

After many long evenings trying and testing buttercream recipes, I finally created the ideal texture that holds its form when piped. This buttercream is perfect for topping cupcakes or coating a celebration cake—and it tastes delicious!

You can add an extra sprinkle of confectioners' sugar to stiffen it or a dash of milk to soften it, depending on the texture you desire. This recipe makes enough buttercream to top 8–10 cupcakes. If you want more for a large cake, simply double or triple the ingredients.

Makes enough to top 8–10 cupcakes

- I cup plus 3 tablespoons (270 g) dairy-free butter/ margarine
- 5 cups (600 g) confectioners' sugar, sifted
- I teaspoon vanilla extract
- Dash of dairy-free milk, if needed

1. Cream the butter or margarine in a bowl for about 3–5 minutes until light and creamy. I use my stand mixer with the balloon-whisk attachment on high speed, but you could use an electric hand mixer or a wooden spoon (though the spoon will take you longer).

2. Add the confectioners' sugar and vanilla extract. Whizz together until fluffy and fully combined. Add a dash of milk if it's too thick.

Keep the buttercream in a sealed container in the fridge for up to a week until you are ready to use it. Bring it up to room temperature and re-whip it before using if it's been in the fridge.

American-Style Chocolate Buttercream

Cocoa transforms a plain buttercream base into a sumptuous chocolaty frosting—this buttercream perfectly complements any cupcake or celebration cake!

This recipe makes enough buttercream to top 8–10 cupcakes. If you want more for a large cake, simply double or triple the ingredients.

Makes enough to top 8–10 cupcakes

- 1 cup plus 1½ tablespoons (250 g) dairy-free butter/margarine
- 3⅔ cups (445 g) confectioners' sugar, sifted
- 4 heaped tablespoons cocoa powder
- Dash of dairy-free milk, if needed

1. Cream the butter or margarine in a bowl for about 3–5 minutes—I use my stand mixer with the balloon-whisk attachment on high speed, but you could use an electric hand mixer or a wooden spoon (though the spoon will take you longer).

2. Add the confectioners' sugar and cocoa powder and mix until creamy. Add a dash of milk if it's too thick.

Use the buttercream right away or keep it in the fridge in a sealed container for up to a week. Bring it to room temperature and re-whip it before using if it's been in the fridge.

Honeycomb

This is a really fun recipe to make, as the baking soda reacts with the other ingredients to fizz and rise as it turns from a liquid to a solid in front of your eyes! Use this vegan honeycomb as a tasty snack, dunk it in chocolate to create chocolate-covered honeycomb bars, or crumble it into or onto cakes to decorate.

Makes a block of honeycomb 9 by 7 inches and 2 inches deep (23 by 18 cm and 5 cm deep)

- 6 tablespoons (125 g) golden syrup
- 1 cup (200 g) superfine sugar
- 2 tablespoons water
- 3½ teaspoons baking soda
- Bar of dairy-free dark chocolate, melted (optional)

1. Line a 9-by-7-inch (23 by 18 cm) deep baking pan with parchment paper (see page 17 for how to line a baking pan). Allow the paper to hang on either side of the pan—this will make it easier to remove the honeycomb.

2. Place the syrup, superfine sugar, and water in a medium or large saucepan over medium-high heat.

3. After a few minutes, the sugar will begin to melt. Use a wooden spoon to stir the mixture, being very careful not to get it on your skin, as hot sugar will burn! Keep stirring to keep it from sticking.

4. It's best to use a candy thermometer for this step. You're looking for the mixture to reach 149°C (300°F) which is known as the "hard crack" stage, as it gives the honeycomb crunch.

5. Once it's reached the desired temperature, turn off the heat and stir in the baking soda immediately. The mixture will begin to rise and bubble, so be quick (and be very careful not to get any on your skin).

6. Once combined, immediately pour the mixture into the lined pan—DO NOT spread out or level, or it will lose all of its air bubbles. The honeycomb will bubble and rise in the pan.

7. Once the honeycomb has settled, place the pan or dish in a cool room to set. This will take about 1 hour. DO NOT touch it before it has set! Once it's cool and hard, break into shards and dunk into melted dark chocolate, if using.

Store in a sealed container at room temperature and eat within a few days of making.

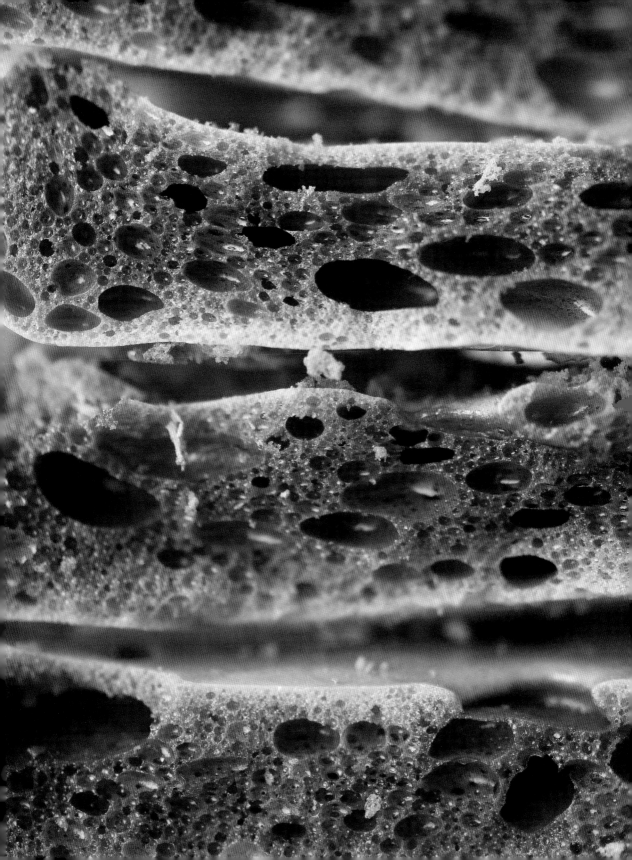

Lemon Curd

It can be difficult to find vegan lemon curd in supermarkets, as most traditional versions contain eggs. Here, I've created a simple recipe that tastes just as delicious as its eggy counterpart: it's so good, you'll want to grab a spoon and eat it straight out of the jar. Use this lemon curd to top pancakes, scones, and waffles; spread it between cake layers; or use it as a delicious lemon filling in macarons—the possibilities are endless.

Makes 1 cup (280 g)

- 2 tablespoons cornstarch
- 2 tablespoons water
- ⅓ cup (70 g) dairy-free butter/margarine
- ⅓ cup plus 1 tablespoon (80 g) superfine sugar
- ⅓ cup plus 1½ tablespoons (100 ml) lemon juice (from 3–4 medium lemons)
- ¼ cup (60 g) vegan condensed milk
- Pinch of turmeric, for color (optional)

1. In a small bowl, mix the cornstarch with the water. Stir together to make a paste. Add the paste to a medium saucepan, along with the dairy-free butter or margarine, superfine sugar, lemon juice, condensed milk, and a pinch of turmeric, if using.

2. Place the saucepan on the stove over medium heat, stirring constantly, preferably with a whisk to break up any lumps or a wooden spoon. After 5–8 minutes the lemon curd will thicken. If the curd isn't thickening, turn up the heat and whisk constantly. You will notice the consistency change.

3. You will know it is ready when you drag a wooden spoon along the bottom of the pan and the curd separates and takes a few seconds to come back together. It will thicken up more as it cools.

Once cool, store it in the fridge in a sealed jar/container for up to a week. Before using it, give it a good stir, as it will have thickened.

Swiss Meringue Buttercream

Swiss meringue buttercream is silky smooth and is lighter and less sweet than regular buttercream or American frosting. Traditionally, egg whites are used in this recipe, but you can make an excellent vegan version using aquafaba. You can add this buttercream to many of your bakes and desserts.

Makes enough to top 18 cupcakes or to frost a small celebration cake

- ¾ cup plus 2 tablespoons (200 g) dairy-free block butter (not margarine)
- 2½ cups (300 g) confectioners' sugar, sifted
- 1 teaspoon vanilla extract
- ¼ cup plus 1 tablespoon (70 ml) aquafaba

HOLLY'S TIP

Swiss meringue buttercream will stiffen up when chilled, so before serving, allow it to come to room temperature.

1. Using a stand mixer with a balloon-whisk attachment or an electric hand mixer, whip the butter until creamy.

2. Sift in the confectioners' sugar and vanilla extract, and whip on high speed for a couple of minutes to incorporate it.

3. Pour in the aquafaba and whip for 5 minutes until it turns light and creamy. Be careful not to overwhip or it can become too soft. If it does, just add in more confectioners' sugar until it is thick and creamy. The buttercream should be thick, very creamy, and silky smooth. It's now ready to use on cakes, cupcakes, or other confections.

Store in a sealed container in the fridge. Use within 2 days of making. When you want to use the buttercream, re-whip it, then transfer it to a piping bag fitted with a nozzle of your choice.

This recipe is for a vanilla-flavored buttercream, but you can make it chocolate flavored by adding ¾ cup plus 3 tablespoons (150 g) melted dark chocolate. Just whip everything up as in the instructions above but without the vanilla extract, then add the melted chocolate and whip that in until it is fully incorporated.

Royal Icing

Royal icing hardens at room temperature, making it perfect for decorating cookies, cakes, gingerbread houses, and more. I've created a simple vegan version using aquafaba that works every time and tastes great, too. Add a few drops of vegan gel food coloring to your mixture to create royal icing of all different colors.

Ready-made aquafaba can be bought from the supermarket, or you can simply use the liquid from a can of chickpeas.

Makes enough to ice around 20 medium sugar cookies

- ⅓ cup plus I tablespoon (90 ml) aquafaba
- I teaspoon vanilla extract
- 4⅓ cups (520 g) confectioners' sugar, sifted

1. Whisk the aquafaba using either an electric hand mixer or a stand mixer with the balloon-whisk attachment on high speed until frothy—this usually takes around 5 minutes.

2. Add the vanilla extract and confectioners' sugar and whisk together until it holds a stiff peak.

3. Use right away or transfer it to a sealed container and keep it in the fridge for up to a few weeks (see Tip).

HOLLY'S TIP

If the icing has been stored in the fridge, give it a stir before use. This will loosen it and make it creamier to work with.

Chocolate Ganache

I've created this heavenly chocolate ganache to be used in a variety of recipes. You could use it to fill truffles, pastries, or layer cakes, or as a topping on cupcakes, tarts, and cookies—there are so many ways to enjoy my ganache and take your bake to the next level!

Makes 1⅓ cups (330 g)

- ¾ cup plus 3 tablespoons (150 g) dairy-free chocolate chips or chunks
- ¾ cups plus 1½ tablespoons (200 g) dairy-free cream

HOLLY'S TIP

Add more cream for a creamier, silkier ganache.

1. Place the chocolate and cream in a medium saucepan over medium heat and simmer, stirring continuously, until the chocolate has melted and is glossy.

You can use the ganache right away or let it cool down for a thicker consistency. Store in a sealed container in the fridge, where it will last for up to 4 days. You may need to leave it out for 15 minutes and mix again to make it softer after it has been in the fridge.

Four-Ingredient Chocolate Hazelnut Spread

I could honestly eat chocolate spread by the spoonful, straight from the jar. This simple recipe makes a delicious Nutella-inspired, four-ingredient chocolate spread flavored with hazelnuts. Use in cupcakes, spread it on waffles or toast, melt it inside crêpes—get creative with it. You will need a high-speed blender to get the best results.

Makes ¾ cup (195 g)

- ¾ cup (100 g) whole raw hazelnuts
- ¾ cup (120 g) dairy-free dark chocolate
- ¼ cup (30 g) confectioners' sugar, sifted
- ½ teaspoon vanilla extract

1. Preheat the oven to 400°F (200°C) and line a baking sheet with parchment paper (see page 17 for how to line a baking sheet). Lay out the hazelnuts on the baking sheet and roast them for 10 minutes—this helps to release their natural oils and loosen their skins (and also makes them easier to blend).

2. Remove the hazelnuts from the oven and set them aside to cool slightly, then transfer them to a clean tea towel. Gently rub the nuts with the towel to remove the skins (they don't all have to be perfectly skin-free).

3. Place the hazelnuts in a small high-speed blender and blend until a butter forms—this will take around 10 minutes. Stop the blender a few times and scrape down the sides to make sure all the nuts get blended.

4. Melt the chocolate using a bain-marie (see page 17) or in the microwave. Add the melted chocolate, confectioners' sugar, and vanilla extract to the blender with the nuts, and blend until combined and smooth. If your chocolate spread isn't sweet enough, just add more confectioners' sugar.

Store in a sealed container at room temperature (if stored in the fridge it will harden) and use within a week of making.

Berry Jam

You only need two ingredients to create a great-tasting fruit jam that's full of flavor and tang. This is a truly versatile jam that can be used in and added to so many recipes in this book—for example, the jam-filled cookies (see page 122), the strawberry trifles (see page 154), or the strawberry cupcakes (see page 66). If you can't get hold of jam sugar, superfine sugar will give great results too. I prefer to use frozen berries for a thicker consistency and a sharper taste.

Makes about ½ cup (115 g)

- 1⅓ cups (200 g) frozen berries (for example, raspberries, strawberries, blackberries, or blueberries)
- ⅓ cup (60 g) jam sugar or superfine sugar

1. Place the frozen berries in a medium saucepan and add the sugar.

2. Place over medium-high heat and bring to a boil. Simmer for 10–15 minutes, stirring occasionally with a wooden spoon or spatula until thickened. Make sure the jam doesn't burn or stick to the pan.

3. Take off the heat and allow to cool. It will thicken as it cools.

Once cool, store in a clean, sealed container or jar in the fridge for up to a few weeks.

Caramel Sauce

My simple three-ingredient caramel sauce is sweet, gooey, and buttery, and it transforms any recipe it touches—for example, my salted caramel tartlets (see page 166), sticky toffee pudding (see page 151), or drizzled over my American-style pancakes (see page 169). The possibilities are endless!

Makes 1 cup (245 g)

- ¾ cup plus 2½ table-spoons (180 g) superfine sugar
- ¼ cup (60 g) dairy-free cream
- ¼ cup (60 ml) dairy-free milk

HOLLY'S TIP

To make salted caramel sauce, add ½ teaspoon of sea salt at the end when it is still hot.

1. Get all your ingredients ready before you start. Place the superfine sugar into a medium pan over low-medium heat, stirring continuously with a wooden spoon or whisk for 5–8 minutes until the sugar melts. Make sure it doesn't burn.

2. When the sugar has completely melted and is golden, turn off the heat. Leave for a few seconds, then carefully add the cream and immediately stir vigorously. It will steam and bubble, but keep stirring.

3. When the caramel starts to cool down, stir in the milk. Place the pan back over low-medium heat and bring it back to a boil. It will begin to bubble—keep stirring for another 1–2 minutes.

4. Turn off the heat and pour the sauce into a heatproof container. Once cool, place in the fridge to set. It will thicken as it cools.

You can store the caramel sauce in an airtight container in the fridge for up to a few weeks. It can be reheated to ensure that it is easier to pour. You can do this by placing the container in a pan of boiling water for a few minutes. Just make sure that the container is heatproof. If it isn't, you will need to transfer the sauce to a heatproof container before reheating it.

How to Temper Chocolate

Tempering is a technique for setting melted chocolate that keeps it from easily melting on your fingers and gives an even, glossy finish that will elevate your bakes to the next level. You can use tempered chocolate to create decorative and tasty chocolate bark or to make chocolate curls like the ones on top of the chocolate celebration cake (see page 35).

Professional bakers often use a candy thermometer when tempering chocolate, but you can do it without one. This is the method I use when tempering without a thermometer:

1. Weigh the amount of chocolate required for the recipe and cut or break it into small chunks.

2. Make a bain-marie by half-filling a small saucepan with water and placing a heatproof bowl on top (make sure that the bowl sits comfortably and doesn't touch the water).

3. Place three-quarters of the chocolate in the heatproof bowl, holding back one-quarter, as this is required later.

4. Melt the chocolate using the bain-marie (see page 17) over medium heat, stirring occasionally with a spatula or heatproof spoon. When it is almost fully melted, take the pan off the heat but keep stirring until all the chocolate has melted.

5. Pour the melted chocolate into a separate heatproof bowl. Add the remaining chocolate a little at a time, stirring quickly as you do so (this is to bring down the temperature of the chocolate).

6. The chocolate will start to thicken. To check if the chocolate is ready, dip a clean spoon into the chocolate, then remove it and see how long it takes for the chocolate on the spoon to harden—it should harden within a couple of minutes. This shows that the chocolate is ready and tempered.

7. If there are some chunks of chocolate that are still not fully melted, remove them at this point, as you don't want to overwork it.

8. The chocolate is now ready to use in your recipe, but you will need to work quickly, as it will harden quite rapidly.

How to Decorate Cookies and Gingerbread

You will need:

- Cookies (see page 147)
- Royal icing (see page 200)
- Gel food coloring (rather than liquid)
- Bowls
- Toothpicks
- Spoons
- Piping bags and tips
- Scissors
- Water

LINE AND FLOOD ICINGS

Line icing is what creates an outline around the edge of a cookie, making a barrier for you to fill with smooth flood icing while preventing it from seeping out. Line icing should be a similar texture to toothpaste: thick yet easy to pipe.

Flood icing is a thinned-out version of line icing, used to fill in the cookies and give a background color. It should be thin enough that it smooths out on its own but not so thin that it drips off the edges of your cookies.

1. Arrange the cookies in front of you on a clean kitchen worktop.

2. Start off with the line icing. Put around 3 tablespoons (or however much you think you may need for the borders and the line detailing) of royal icing into a small bowl. Mix in a drop of gel food coloring. I use a toothpick to add a tiny amount at a time to get the right shade. Place the icing in a piping bag fitted with a small round-tip nozzle, or snip off the tip of a disposable piping bag. This line icing will create the outlines and detailing on your cookies. Repeat this process to make as many colors as you require, leaving the leftover icing for the flood icing.

3. To create the outline on your cookie, hold the piping bag at a right angle to the cookie and allow the icing to fall from the piping bag as you draw a line around the edge of the cookies. Make sure not to leave any gaps; otherwise, the flood icing may seep out.

4. When you've finished all of the outlines, make the flood icing. Divide the leftover royal icing into enough small bowls for however many colors you need. Add the colors you require with a toothpick as you did before, but this time also add a drop of water. Mix until the icing is soft enough to flood the cookies.

Recipe continued on page 210

5. Transfer the flood icing to separate piping bags fitted with small round-tip nozzles, or snip the tips off disposable piping bags if you don't have the nozzles. Pipe the icing into the middle of the cookie, or wherever you want to fill with the color. Then, using a toothpick, spread it out evenly. Shake the cookie lightly to make sure all the gaps are filled and the icing is level.

6. Once the cookies have a background color, let the icing set (this will take several hours) before working on the details.

7. Once the icing has set, use the thicker line icing again to create the details. After decorating the cookies, leave them to dry on a flat surface at room temperature. Drying time depends on the thickness of the icing—it could take up to 24 hours.

8. If you want to make individual icing decorations to add to the cookies, pipe the decorations onto parchment paper and let them set at room temperature before applying them to the cookies. Apply with a tiny bit of the royal icing, as this will set the decoration in place.

How to Frost a Cake

Buttercream is a kind of frosting made using butter or margarine with confectioners' sugar and is great for all cakes. Cream cheese frosting is made with cream cheese and confectioners' sugar instead of butter or margarine. Some of my recipes include both butter/margarine and cream cheese. Swiss meringue buttercream is lighter and silkier than traditional buttercream frosting.

Tools for perfectly frosting a cake

- **Cake scraper:** helps to smooth out the buttercream or frosting on the cake.

- **Cake turntable:** a revolving cake stand that helps you to achieve an even spread of frosting and makes frosting a cake easier and faster.

- **Piping bag:** a cone-shaped bag made from cloth or plastic that is used to squeeze buttercream/ frosting onto baked goods and is often used with a piping tip/nozzle.

- **Piping tip/nozzle:** a nozzle that can be fitted to the piping bag. You can get various sizes that create different frosting designs.

HOLLY'S TIP

Never frost a warm cake. Allow your cake to cool fully before frosting; otherwise, it can result in an uneven finish with melted buttercream or frosting.

FILLING AND LAYERING

1. I find it best to frost a cake on a cake board, as it makes it easier to transfer your finished cake to a stand or serving plate. If you don't have a cake board or a cake turntable, you can just use a flat plate and turn it by hand. If you do have a cake board, stick it to the turntable using a small amount of buttercream or frosting. Place a cake layer in the center of your board or plate, and stick it in place with a little buttercream or frosting. Make sure you have enough buttercream or frosting for the filling, the crumb coat, the final coat, and any decoration.

2. For the filling, make sure that your buttercream or frosting is fairly firm so the cakes don't slide about when you're working on them. Fill a piping bag fitted with a large round-tip nozzle with your chosen buttercream or frosting. If you don't have a nozzle, you can snip the end off a disposable piping bag. If you don't have a piping bag, you can use an offset spatula to fill the cake and smooth it out, but I find that using the piping bag ensures each layer is completely even and creates a more stable cake.

3. Pipe a ring of buttercream or frosting around the edge of the cake and fill the middle with a spiral of the buttercream or frosting. If you're using a spatula, spread an even amount of the buttercream or frosting over the top of the cake layer. Use a small offset spatula to level and smooth out the buttercream or frosting. It should be as even and flat as possible—this will result in a level cake.

4. Place another cake layer on top of the buttercream or frosting and very gently press it down to secure the cake. Don't press too firmly, or you risk breaking the cakes. Look at the cake from different angles to make sure it's level. If the cake is slipping off to one side, use your hands to ease it into the middle.

Recipe continued on page 212

- **Large spatula or palette knife:** helps to spread the frosting onto the cake.

- **Offset spatula:** a spatula that has a bend in the metal. I prefer to use one of these when working with buttercream or frosting.

- **Cake dowel:** a rigid support made from wood or plastic that adds extra support to your cake, especially when making tiered/layered cakes.

HOLLY'S TIP

Hold the cake scraper or knife vertically. This helps to prevent any unwanted lines in the buttercream or frosting and ensures a smooth finish.

HOLLY'S TIP

Remember to wipe any buttercream or frosting off your tools before smoothing the cake.

5. Repeat until you have used all the cake layers. To add security to the cake and prevent it from leaning, you can press a dowel into the center. Make sure to cut it to size, as you don't want it to stick up out of the cake.

CRUMB COAT

1. A crumb coat is really important for a clean-looking cake because it locks in all the loose cake crumbs. This means that, when it comes to applying the final layer, you're not dragging crumbs through the buttercream or frosting. A "naked cake" is when the initial crumb coat is the final coat.

2. Scoop up some of the buttercream or frosting with a spatula and spread it all over the sides and top of the cake, filling in any cracks or holes as you go. You don't need a lot of frosting, just a thin layer to lock in the crumbs. Use one hand to hold the spatula, applying the buttercream, and the other to gently spin the turntable or plate. Use a cake scraper or palette knife to scrape the buttercream or frosting so it is smooth. Discard any excess, as it may contain crumbs.

3. When the cake has a thin and even layer of buttercream or frosting, place it in the fridge and allow the crumb coat to set for about an hour. If you don't allow it to set, when you apply the final layer, the buttercream or frosting may slide around.

FINAL COAT

1. When the buttercream or frosting feels firm to the touch, remove the cake from the fridge and apply the final coat. Apply a thick layer of the buttercream or frosting over the entire cake as you rotate the turntable.

2. Using an offset spatula, smooth the frosting on top of the cake so that it's level. Then use a cake scraper (or a large spatula or palette knife if you don't have a scraper) to smooth the sides of the cake, scraping the excess buttercream or frosting off the cake scraper after each scrape.

3. If you notice any gaps or imperfections in your cake, simply fill them in with buttercream or frosting and use the cake scraper, spatula, or palette knife to smooth them out.

After you have given the cake its final coat, you can leave it plain or decorate. Check out my website, www.thelittleblogofvegan.com, for more techniques.

More Inspiration

For more of my bakes, visit my website (www.thelittleblogofvegan.com). You can also find me on Instagram, Facebook, Twitter, and Pinterest—all social media links are on my website. You can also get some exclusive content sent directly to your inbox if you sign up for my newsletter—details are on my website. Here are some of my favorite recipes from my blog.

THE ESSENTIAL BOOK OF VEGAN BAKES

MORE INSPIRATION

Thank You

To my family: I can genuinely say I have the best family in the world. The support, laughter, and love I get from you is like no other. I love you all so much!

To my mom: I don't know where I'd be without you. You are my rock, my everything, my best friend, and you have been there for me since day one (in life and on my blogging journey). This book wouldn't exist if it wasn't for your incredible help. You have worked so hard, and I can't thank you enough—I owe you so much. You've helped me to navigate my book journey, tested recipes with me, and have been there to offer lots of positive encouragement throughout. I love you to the moon and back. Best mom ever!

To my dad (the best dad in the world!): You provide me with endless laughs, and you're always the first in line to taste-test lemon cakes or pastries. You're the main person I call upon for a quick shopping trip if I've run out of something, and you're always ready to give your culinary advice. Most of the berry- or lemon-flavored bakes in this book are for you, Dad.

To my sister, Naomi Victoria, a content creator and my best friend: We have so much in common and support one another in our work. It was you who named my blog and encouraged me right at the beginning. I have endless gratitude to you for that and for helping me get to where I am today. I love you!

To my cat, my Tiggy, my guardian angel: You showed me love and compassion and taught me how amazing animals are. I owe being vegan to you, my boy, so thank you from the bottom of my heart. From being with me while I baked in the kitchen to sitting with me while I edited my work, you've always been there to guide me through. I miss you with all my heart. This book is dedicated to Tiggy, as I wouldn't be where I am today if it wasn't for him.

To Amanda Preston, my literary agent: The biggest thank you for taking me on for my first baking book and for being so kind and supportive.

The whole team at Ebury Publishing has been incredible and extremely accommodating. I wish to thank them for making one of my dreams come true.

- Celia Palazzo, Emily Brickell, and Tamsin English, my editors and points of contact at Ebury.
- Lucy Sykes-Thompson, my book designer at Ebury.
- Serena Nazareth, for overseeing all production aspects of the project at Ebury.

I would also like to give a particular mention to the US team members at Countryman Press, including Isabel McCarthy (editor), Devon Zahn (production manager), Allison Chi (designer), Jessica Murphy (managing editor), Devorah Backman (marketing manager), and Rina Garcia (publicist).

And to all my family, friends, and neighbors who have been official recipe testers.

This book wouldn't exist if it weren't for my amazing followers, who have supported me since day one. From every single kind comment and supportive direct message to re-creating my recipes and sharing your feedback and photos—it all means the world to me.

Dedication

I am dedicating my first baking book to my cat, Tiggs.

He was the reason I went vegan, as he inspired my love and compassion for animals. He was by my side throughout most of my life, growing up, and all through my blogging journey. He inspired many of my animal-themed bakes that are featured on my website and social media. He was with me and comforted me when I was going through a tough time (see why in my story on page 8). He would always make me smile, and I never felt alone when he was around. If I hadn't become vegan, *The Little Blog of Vegan* would never have been created, so I have a lot to thank him for.

Apart from him being the most loving, adorable, softest, photogenic, and intelligent cat in the world, he was also my baking buddy and would always be around to see what I was doing. He would sit with me while I was editing photos and would always get involved in any PR deliveries (he would literally get inside the boxes and play around!). He was the best fur-friend anyone could have asked for, and not a day goes by that I don't think about him or miss his presence, especially while I'm working.

I promised him that I would make him proud and write a baking book. He was watching me when some of the photos for this book were taken, so I have extremely fond memories of them all. I just wish I could have shown him this book, but I know he's looking down on me now with pride.

I am so grateful to Ebury for allowing me to dedicate this book to Tiggs. It means the absolute world to me.

Tiggs, my boy 2002–2020

Index

First published as The Little Book of Vegan Bakes in 2022 by Ebury Press.
Ebury Press is part of the Penguin Random House group of companies.

For information about permission to reproduce selections from this book, write to
Permissions, Countryman Press, 500 Fifth Avenue, New York, NY 10110

For information about special discounts for bulk purchases, please contact
W. W. Norton Special Sales at specialsales@wwnorton.com or 800-233-4830

Manufacturing by Versa Press
Production manager: Devon Zahn

Countryman Press
www.countrymanpress.com

An imprint of W. W. Norton & Company, Inc.
500 Fifth Avenue, New York, NY 10110
www.wwnorton.com

978-1-68268-739-0

10 9 8 7 6 5 4 3 2 1